The Guide to
Truly Effective Cycling

The Guide to Truly Effective Cycling

Learn to Self-Coach from BikesEtc Magazine's Cycling Guru

Printed by Kindle Direct Publishing in the United States of America.

First printing, 2019.

Pav Bryan
28236 Via Fierro
Laguna Niguel
92677.

www.spokes.fit

Contents

How to use this guide

This guide has been structured so that you follow a logical journey as you plan and prepare for you training, nutrition and racing. It will never replace a coach as it will not give you an unbiased look at yourself and your training, nor will it hold you accountable, but it will bridge the gap between you not knowing what to do or following hearsay and wishing to pay for 1:1 coaching. If you're just starting on your journey you should start from the beginning. Follow all the steps in the training chapter and you will have exactly what you need in order to get your body ready to complete your goals. The nutrition chapter will ensure that you are fuelling your body well enough to maximise any potential gains from your training. The mentality chapter will ensure that you are training your brain as much as your body, with the final chapter, tactics, being about how to put everything together in the preparation for race day itself. Ideally, you will be reading this before you have started your training but, if not, it should be very easy to adjust your plan to suit the methods covered throughout this book. You should try to read it all before starting and then the book is designed to be convenient to pull out every now and again for ongoing reference.

At the end of each chapter there is a recap heading, tick off each of the points in this recap. Unless you are starting from scratch, you might have ticked some off already, that is ok. You might want to review yours to make sure they align with what you've learnt. Either way, they are in the most logical order for you to make the most from self-coaching.

If you don't have one already, I recommend you setup a TrainingPeaks account[i]. The basic version is free and the features that come with the premium version will save you a lot of time and effort. I reference TrainingPeaks throughout this book as I believe it to be the most effective platform to use to plan your training, however, you can complete all the recap points on other platforms, spreadsheets or even pen and paper.

Introduction

The Guide to Truly Effective Cycling was born out of the accompanying information I send to my clients. I believe that, no matter the level of your existing knowledge and understanding of how the human body works, this guide will help you to better understand the methodology behind your training, to make the most of it and to achieve your potential.

In my experience, when my clients understand the methodology behind their training programme, they switch from half-engaged to fully-engaged and, in doing so, they are then equipped to do absolutely everything they can to succeed. However, this guide is not designed to replace what a professional coach can offer you; he or she will see what you do not see, be able to make unbiased and objective decisions, plus have skills and experience that might far outweigh what you can learn yourself—many coaches are themselves coached for these reasons.

Sometimes, it is all too easy to be so caught up with your own training programme that you fail to see the bigger picture. For example, you might set yourself a training plan and then decide you don't want to train on the day you have planned. It's easy to take the easy route out when you write your own plan. It's even easier to change it at the last minute, at which point everything becomes unstructured riding; not training. Finally, you may find yourself training solely towards B or C goals to the detriment of the A goal.

Another advantage of having a professional coach to help you is accountability. Having someone to hold you accountable for what you are supposed to be doing is a massive motivator, and once you start paying for something you will want to get the most from it. A coach will reassure you when things go wrong, celebrate with you when things go right, and push you over that plateau alongside identifying problems that you may not see.

Finally, if you plan to go it alone, you also need to be aware that unless you are able to devise an effective training plan and remain 100% dedicated to it, you still may not get the same results as a coached rider.

I believe there are three key components to improving your cycling performance: training, nutrition and mentality. And, in my experience, there is a clear split ratio, with training sitting around 15%, nutrition at around 35% and mental capacity making up the remaining 50%. I have therefore found that it is far more important to pay attention to conditioning your state of mind and your behaviour than to concentrate solely on training. However, without all three, gains are just not possible. We will be exploring all three in detail.

Truly Personal Coaching

I pioneered the Truly Personal Coaching methodology.

In a world where coaches traditionally place the end goal at the centre of their practises, I choose to make it client-centric. Rather than giving my clients a programme that will get them to their goals in any manner, I prefer to ensure that each person's individual circumstances are taken into account, as they work towards obtaining their goal.

In the beginning, I had a simpler version of this, which many coaches now follow. Making training work for the client, factoring in influences like the amount of time that someone has available, or how stressful, both physically and mentally, their job is.

Truly Personal Coaching is an evolution of this methodology asking the client how they want to achieve their goal, what their commitment is likely to be and how much they are willing to sacrifice. When asked this, the majority of people want to enjoy the journey towards their goal as much as achieving it. Unless you are paid to ride a bike, you might always prioritise enjoyment above all else; this is where a lot of coaching loses its personal touch, and why I have such a high retention rate with my clients and why they consistently rate my service above others.

Part One
Training
'It never gets easier; you just go faster' (Greg LeMond)

Chapter One
Definitions - Components of fitness

There are various systems to describe the different components of fitness, usually depending on where you are in the world. If you are in the US, you may find that some of the terminology is slightly different to those who are in the UK. As a British Cycling trained coach, I will describe the types of training using the British Cycling[ii] methodology. It's worth mentioning that the US version, the terms mainly coined by coaches such as Joe Friel, Hunter Allen and Dr. Andy Coggan, is very similar but has subtle differences that may cause confusion. For example, muscular endurance in the US refers more to upper aerobic endurance work (simply called endurance in the US), whereas short term muscular endurance is the term used for explosive but short bursts of power in the UK. As you can see, these different systems may cause confusion.

Here's my attempt at translating the components of fitness, might come in handy later! Read on for a more comprehensive view at what each one actually is.

Speed - The British Cycling definition of speed is not anything to do with velocity, it's actually referring to speed skill, also known as cadence work or simply leg speed! It is the ability, or flexibility, to spin one's legs at a faster rate. At some point in your cycling training you should always train this, it can be especially important if you are looking to improve efficiency, recovery or sprinting, among many other goals.

Strength - If you are British, you might refer to strength as on or off the bike work. If you're American, you might refer to this as purely off the bike, and call on the bike strength work force. Either way, when talking about this it is the act of building greater strength in your body. Like speed, strength should always be trained at some point in your year, but might be especially important if you are looking to do hilly rides, track or many other goals.

Aerobic Endurance - Defined as any longer sustained effort where the body is continually able to supply energy and oxygen. It can be split into further sub-categories. Base work might indicate the lower intensity of this component of fitness, whereas muscular endurance, speed work or even power sessions are common for the higher intensity. This is commonly trained for all disciplines of cycling, although the intensity of this will be indicated by what your goals are and how much time you have available.

Anaerobic Endurance - Defined as any effort where oxygen isn't present, if you're unclear what this might be it is typically short sharp blurts, such as sprints or gym work. This might be one of the only commonly similar terms, however, it might be referred to as VO2 training as well. Again, this is something that you will need to train at some point in your year. If you follow standard periodisation, this will be near to your target event and reverse periodisation this might be more off-season.

Sprinting - Peak muscular power, peak power, power, all names that might be referring to sprinting. You might not target this type of training if you're not going to be doing any sprinting in your target event, but you could still include some efforts like this in your training, good to freshen it up and you might get good cross component of fitness adaptation too. Sprinting is typically one of the more enjoyable areas of cycling.

Short Term Muscular Endurance - This one can be tricky as American's will refer to upper aerobic endurance work as muscular endurance. British Cycling refers to STME as shorter, still sustained, bursts of power which might look like a hill climb or bridging a gap between groups, which predominantly might be anaerobic. American's might simply call this power work. Like I just mentioned, you will be training this almost regardless of your target, it'll be unlikely your event won't include some form of short, sustainable, burst of power!

Hopefully that'll come in use! Let's now move onto the individual components of fitness.

British Cycling training grids

Training Zone	Purpose	%MHR	%MMP	RPE (1-10)/How you feel	Duration
Recovery	Regeneration and Recovery	< 60	< 35	1 Very relaxed. Able to carry on a conversation.	< 60'
1. Basic	Establish base endurance	60-65	35-45	2 Relaxed. Able to carry on a conversation.	90'-360'
2.Basic	Improve efficiency	65-75	45-55	3 Working. Feel warmer. Heart rate and respiration up. May sweat.	60'-240'
3.Intensive	Improve sustainable power	75-82	55-65	5 Hard work. Heart rate and respiration up. Carbon dioxide build-up. Sweating. Breathing hard.	45'-120'
4.Intensive	Push threshold up	82-89	65-75	6 Stressed. Panting. Sweating freely.	30'-60'
5.Maximal	Sustain a high percentage of maximal aerobic power	89-94	75-85	7 Very stressed. Gasping. Sweating heavily.	14'-40'
6.Maximal	Increase maximum power output	> 94	85-100	10 heavily stressed. Gasping. Sweating heavily.	4'-10' intervals
Supra-maximal	Increase sprint power output	N/A	> 100	10 extremely stressful. Gasping. Sweating heavily.	Short intervals

Training Zone	Purpose	Physiological Adaptations	Race fitness
Recovery	Regeneration and recovery	Increase blood flow to muscles to flush out waste products and provide nutrients	Promotes recovery and therefore training response
Zone 1	Establish base endurance	Improves fat metabolism, gets muscles/tendons/ligaments/nerves used to cycling. Increases economy	More efficient use of energy. Prepares body for harder training, works on technique/skill
Zone 2	Improve efficiency	Improves the ability to use oxygen, produce power and increases efficiency	Able to produce more power with the same level of effort, works on technique/skill
Zone 3	Improve sustainable power	Improves carbohydrate metabolism, changes some fast twitch muscle to slow-twitch	Improved sustainable power, good for all cycling events
Zone 4	Push threshold up	Improves carbohydrate metabolism, develops lactate threshold, changes some fast twitch muscle to slow-twitch	Improved sustainable race pace, useful during tapering or pre-competition periods: too much time in this zone can cause staleness
Zone 5	Sustain a high percentage of maximal aerobic power	Develops cardiovascular system and VO2max, improves anaerobic energy production and speeds turnover of waste products	Improved time trialling ability and resistance to short-term fatigue
Zone 6	Increase maximum power output		
Supra-maximal	Increase sprint power output	Increases maximum muscle power, develops neural control of pedalling at specific cadence	Develop race-specific skills at race pace, starting power, sprint speed, and the ability to jump away from the bunch

Aerobic endurance: zones 1-4

Aerobic endurance is when you are able to continuously transport oxygen throughout your body for long periods of time. Using the zonal system set by Maximum Minute Power (MMP) this would be identified in zones 1-4. It's important to note that, regardless of how you set or define your zones, there will be some cross-over. The variation can be limited by the use of a power meter, but there will be points where you will get adaptation typically seen when training in one zone whilst actually being in another. Fatigue will also play a factor in this sort of training as the more tired you become the less effective zonal training will become. Each range will produce a slightly different adaptation in your body but zones 1-4 are all aerobic.

The lower zones 1 and 2 are very easy zones. As the grid suggests an hour minimum is needed to train in these two zones, it could be less if you're new to cycling or have recently returned to cycling after injury. The more trained you are; the longer zone 1 or 2 rides will need to be. My advice is that these two zones need to be maintained at a steady pace, so you need to keep stops to a minimum—a flatter route will help to keep you in the prescribed zones. Whilst club rides are great motivators during spells of bad weather, be aware that this can be detrimental to zonal training since you might end up stopping too much or, more likely, riding too hard.

The higher zones 3 and 4 will be harder work. You'll need to ease yourself into these if you are not used to it, have had a break from training or are coming back from injury. It can be fatiguing, and your body will need time to get used to it. Intervals are common the more intense you get, and you will need to allow recovery time between each effort so you can sustain the higher intensity for longer periods overall. The grid shows a total time I'd recommend you train, but this is not necessary interval length. I would suggest that as a guide the top of zone 4 would also be approximately your Functional Threshold Power (FTP) or the highest amount of power you could sustain continuously for an hour. However, as I mentioned earlier, there may be some cross-over.

Anaerobic threshold: zone 5
As the name suggests, this is where your body stops using oxygen in the process of fuelling your body and the duration at which you can sustain this intensity starts to rapidly drop. This is particularly hard training; intervals might be the best way to train this zone.

The grid shows the maximum duration I'd recommend you spend in entirety in this zone. You might have a considerable amount of recovery time in between intervals in order to ensure each one is stronger. As you get used to training in this zone you could reduce recovery time as a method of progression.

I would suggest that all of or part of your best 20-minute effort would sit in this zone, although you might not actually be anaerobic for all of it. You might also expect to do a short prologue time trial within this zone. Hill climbs when riding normally or during a race might also be in this zone.

Short term muscular endurance: zone 6
This is the biggest difference in terminology between the UK and US methodology. Short Term Muscular Endurance (STME) as part of the UK method refers to a very brief period of time where you sustain a higher amount of power. The US method suggests STME is a higher aerobic endurance. If you use FTP to set your zones, you might consider the US version of STME to be Sweet-Spot (SS) training. For me, STME would be your zone 6 area. The top end would be the most you could sustain for three minutes, although not much else would happen immediately after! Then below that, you'd drop intensity and sustain the effort for longer.

You will be in this zone for most hill climb time trials or if you are breaking away or bridging a gap you'll probably start in this zone before settling into one below. To train this you'll use intervals;

you could do hill reps, jumps (very hard but short sprint-like efforts to build explosive power) or attack intervals (more sustained, maybe three minutes but at a very high intensity), which is where you may be thinking about how you will break away in a road race—an incredibly intense effort with the aim of getting a gap, and so on. Make it specific to your event. Add in plenty of recovery in between each interval so that they are all completed well.

The point at which your performance drops so much that it is no longer worth continuing is often a point for discussion, I'd go with 10%, so if you're aiming for 300 watts then when 270 becomes impossible you could call it a day and focus on being recovered for your next session. Some exceptions to this might be where you are looking to force your body to respond better under fatigue, such as during a last-minute breakaway effort.

Peak Muscle Power (PMP): Supra-Maximal
PMP is achieved by very short, sharp and hard sprint efforts. You'll probably have a very large amount of recovery time in between so that you can nail each individual one. There might be times when you train in this zone when fatigued to simulate the end of race sprint.

Using MMP you'd see this as anything above your three-minute power output. However, if you're not using power then you might not consider monitoring with heart rate, as your heart rate might struggle to respond quickly enough, instead go by feel (RPE). In terms of RPE, this will feel incredibly hard and you'll only sustain it for a brief period of time, maybe 30 seconds maximum.

Below is a graph that helps explain what you should be doing with duration as you change intensity.

Speed

Speed is a term with a variety of meanings. For me, speed refers to cadence, the rate at which you can spin your legs, or leg speed, rather than a reference to velocity. I quite like the US method of including technique-based training in here (referred to as 'Speed Skill'). Personally, I separate it with clients because I feel that technique-based training can be higher intensity whereas leg speed tends to be lower intensity. When factoring in easier or recovery weeks, a lot of leg speed work can promote recovery and adaptation without stressing the body. Off season is typically a great time to get all these done but consider what your weaknesses are. For example, if you're already an accomplished leg spinner or technically gifted rider, then there will be little point spending too long looking for smaller gains in this respect. Spend your off-season time working your weaknesses, if you tend to grind a low cadence then leg speed is a weakness and you could train it. If you can freely spin your legs then simply use leg speed for easier sessions and recovery, focusing your valuable time working other areas.

Strength

Once the forbidden word within cycling, strength is now one of the most crucial areas where you can get considerable gains. Strength training can be done on or off the bike and is an opportunity to do something different. A lot of people I work with say that it can be a much-needed breath of fresh air.

Be warned, however, that there is a right and a wrong way to approach strength work. In all circumstances, I recommend you consult a qualified personal trainer to ensure you are doing any of the exercises correctly. With the help of a personal trainer—who can give you instructions on a one-to-one basis—you will easily be able to identify specific weaknesses or imbalances in your body. These are incredibly common, even more so for cyclists who spend a considerable amount of time in a position that we simply are not designed to be in!

My advice is to periodise your strength work alongside your cycling. After taking a break you'll want to prepare your body for harder training. This might be the moves you'll do all year around but without any weight. Higher reps will allow your body to get ready for more stimulus later. Think about it like prepping your body, lower weight and higher reps are a base for more to come—jumping in with the heavy weights will shock your body, you might experience severe delayed onset muscle soreness (DOMS) or even injury.

On the bike

On the bike, strength training is pretty much limited to bigger geared efforts. This doesn't have to be your biggest gear, but you need to get your cadence low. It is particularly important that your body is ready for this type of riding. Both a comprehensive warm-up and the necessary previous ground-work on the bike, along with a short phase of light, easier riding, perhaps more focused on leg speed, is a good pre-cursor to adding this in to your plan.

16

The US refers to this component of fitness as Force. Your power might be in zone 3, but your heart rate might not be a reflective monitor of this type of training. It will feel hard, your legs will feel slow, a rough guide is to keep RPM below 60, but this will vary. I would suggest that you always stay seated when doing these intervals, start with a short amount of time and then build up. Staying seated ensures that you are building the muscles correctly and not promoting an imbalance.

Off the bike
As previously mentioned, this is where you can get considerable gains in performance. Start off with a preparation phase of low weight / high reps then, when you're ready, move on to high weight / low rep. I cannot stress highly enough how important it is to ensure you are performing each move correctly and safely. You will need to determine how many weeks you spend training in a maximal (high weight / low rep) way, there are a few methods to do this and you might consider your age, gender and sporting background, but after this point you can switch back to more maintenance of your strength. It's important to note that you do not let strength training affect your cycling training.

As you approach the point where you start to specialise your training to match your target events, you might move back to low weight / high reps, but performed explosively to build power. As you get closer to your target events, you might drop the explosiveness and just look to maintain your off-the-bike strength.

As briefly mentioned above, Delayed Onset Muscle Soreness (DOMS) is common with strength training. Whilst it can be reduced by focusing on recovery factors as described earlier, it's important to be aware that this may have an effect on your other cycling, which is why you'd switch to strength maintenance. How you continue with strength work into the ATP will depend on your circumstance.

Younger people or anyone who builds muscle fast might stop weight training entirely once they get to racing season, however older people or those who struggle to build muscle, might want to weight train year-round and only take time off during the week leading up to an A event.

Flexibility: core
One word—yoga! This will revolutionise your cycling, not just in terms of ability but also in comfort and flexibility. Pilates is very similar to yoga, the main difference being the meditation factor, which varies in yoga from class to class from simple breathing exercises to full on chanting. If you don't like the sound of this, then Pilates may be the way to go, but please do give yoga a try before you dismiss it as you may find that you benefit from it.

To make integrating yoga that little bit easier, you could practice it at home. I'm very aware that incorporating all the ideal aspects of training can rack up a hefty bill! As with strength training, you will see more benefit from a trainer giving you instruction, but doing something in this respect is better than doing nothing and there are some good guides online to help you learn some simple moves that can become an effective session.

Technique
One of the first things you might do after an end of season break is determine what skills or techniques you need to work on in order to reach your goals. Off season is perfect time to develop technique where you can use easier sessions to build on your current ability. I've listed some below, the list is non-exhaustive, and you can check out my blog[iii] and YouTube[iv] channel for help on each specific technique. A coach is a great resource for ensuring you are doing this right. If you are UK based, then your local British Cycling Go-Ride club[v] might have a setup where you can do some skills sessions in a group. 1:1 coaching can be expensive but is certainly going to give you best gains for your money. We provide development of skills and techniques as part of all of our training

plans, we have video guides to help you get started and can analyse videos of yourself, be it climbing or descending—even position on the bike while you're sat on the turbo can be analysed remotely by a competent coach.

Solo skills: climbing, descending, riding no handed (or changing or eating on the bike), cornering, braking, gearing, mounting, dismounting, pedalling efficiency, sprinting, throwing your bike (across the line!), transition (in multi-sport events), track stands.

Group skills: drafting, changing position in a group, leading and following, cornering, bumping (riding in contact with another rider), bunch sprinting.

Recap

1. While you don't need to memorise these, having knowledge of them will save you valuable time when training, not to mention removing any confusion along the way.
2. Bookmark this page or take notes for the following chapters.

Chapter Two
Commitment

One of the most important things that I've introduced—not just to my clients, but perhaps to the coaching world as a whole—is identifying a person's level of commitment. Perhaps there are coaches who determine certain aspects of their clients' training by asking about their commitment levels, but, personally, I'm not aware of any that do. I'm highlighting it here because I find that determining your commitment is a unique way to effectively change the way you train and how much you enjoy your self-coaching experience.

First of all, for most people, there is a specific way in which they might train to reach a common goal. Of course, a professional coach should not just copy and paste a training plan between each client. Sadly, there are some who do, but most will factor in their clients' working patterns and available time. Let's take someone who wants to get better at climbing hills, the best, most direct, route will probably include lots of hill training. But what if that person would rather stay indoors to train? If you simply ignore this and tell them to go outside and then they quit, who here has achieved their goals? The answer is no-one. However, meet this person with their desires and coach this person indoors, give them sessions that target the specific intensities that'll produce the right adaptation to allow them to climb a hill faster and then they actually achieve their goals, who wins? The answer is everyone.

Now I'm not saying that we should ignore the most effective route towards your goals. The hill climb example is one edge of the spectrum. Let's say you want to train for Race Across America (3,000 miles raced from coast to coast of the United States), but you only want to train an hour a day, three days per week. It is unlikely that even the best coaches in the world can produce enough training stimuli to make that happen, you might not even qualify for the event. This type of goal, when taking into account your commitment level, just isn't SMART. In chapter three *(page 28)* we will look into detail exactly what this is.

So, what do you do? Well you need to ask yourself just how committed you are. Don't worry there's no judgement here and you're better off doing it right now than you are getting half way through your training and wanting to quit. You might want to reconsider your goals based on this question. Your goals, if they are going to be very hard for you to achieve, will take a lot of commitment. Are you realistically going to be able to stick to a plan that is completely inflexible, or, are you better off reducing your expectations?

There's no shame in this and here's why. If you train towards a near impossible goal with full commitment, and achieve it, you have succeeded. If you train towards a goal which is entirely possible, yet still challenging, and achieve it, you have still succeeded. If you train towards a goal but give up along the way because you can't stand eating perfectly, training indoors, or anything else, you have not succeeded.

What the commitment question introduces is an element of how much you are willing to deviate from what might be considered the best approach in order to enjoy the journey. Here's some of the more common situations where you might question how committed you are.

Training Scenario
You might think that you would prefer to take the most direct route to in order to reach you goal, and that is fine—you might find that you achieve it effectively if you stick to the plan, however, my personal approach is to determine how often a client trains indoors and how often they train out-of-doors during the summer. For example, you may have been asked by a coach to do interval training indoors on the first sunny day of the year—I wonder whether, in practice, you did actually do that.

Ask yourself whether you will ever want to deviate from the most effective method of training; this might mean you'll be indoors if you are training for a shorter event and therefore spending all summer inside. It might be outdoors, if you are training for a multi-day event and therefore always having to brave the elements, or sitting on the trainer for multiple hours if it gets too bad.

Score yourself out of 10. A 10 here would indicate someone who believes they can follow a rigid plan 100%. This might mean they train indoors more, miss group rides and always commit to doing the most effective training session.

A 1 would indicate you really want flexibility. You will enjoy a free-ride now and again, maybe a club ride is something you want to incorporate into your training and maybe you will ride outside when the sun finally comes out in spring!

You will need to consider exactly what training you will need to do and whether that seems enjoyable to you. You can also think about what you have done in previous years, have you always managed to stick to the plan, or have you been more biased with your training? You might want to revisit this chapter after completing some of the further ones.

Nutrition

Another consideration is how committed you are when it comes to eating. You might achieve your goal quicker by employing an over-strict approach to eating, for example, by not eating out, weighing portions and eating clean 100% of the time. However, if this is not you, you don't think you can manage that and you want to enjoy the journey towards your goals, you will need a much more flexible approach.

A 10 here would indicate someone who is going to follow their nutritional strategy 100%. No deviations, no dinners out (unless you can find somewhere that fits your needs), no treats, no sweets, no desserts, nothing that will compromise your training, very little fun.

A 1 here would indicate someone who is going to do whatever their body or mind feels like. Eating whatever you want without a thought as to what this will do to your performance or your health. Total flexibility.

I imagine you are probably slotting yourself somewhere in between. Be honest. As mentioned above, if you start of too rigid and slip it might be harder to come back from. This is the point to take an objective look at what you have been like previously. Do you have a sweet tooth, do you like the occasional alcoholic drink, do you like to eat out with friends? Plan these in and if you don't think your goal is achievable, have a rethink. Success at a lesser goal is better than failure at a bigger.

Mentality
Ask yourself the question 'does everything I do promote recovery?'. Probably not, almost certainly not if you have an active family with your children. Want to be 100% committed to your goals? Then you can't really play chase with your kid's year around, the effort will be adding stress to your body, and if you're 100% committed you need to be recovering.

Your work might be another big one. If you are active at work, maybe you are a tradesperson or a contractor, would you consider giving up your job in order to be fully committed to training? Probably not.

There are many healthy living scenarios, see chapter 16 *(page 138)*, that you might need to consider now too; can you get enough sleep per night, can you successfully reduce stress and then learn to manage the rest, are you at a high risk of sickness or injury (while not technically something you are committed too, you might want to see if this will derail you), can you commit enough time to relaxation and recovery as you will need and can you reduce external factors well enough to promote your recovery.

This might be the area where most people see themselves dropping a few points. Unless you are a professional athlete, you might simply not have the time or capability to approach this at a commitment level of 10. That is ok, don't give up! You just need to be really honest about whether your goals are achievable.

A 10 here will indicate someone who has time to relax more, a job that is either very accommodating, sedentary or maybe you can take a lot of time off work. You might not have a family, at least not a young one.

A 1 here would indicate someone might need more flexibility (it could come down to a need here, more than a want). The biggest influencers on this are job and family. Please don't ditch either in pursuit of your goals without serious thought, especially your family! The job, perhaps as long as it won't have a negative effect on the rest of your life. I take no responsibility for your actions should you choose to do this...!

Again, you're probably slotting yourself somewhere between, perhaps this is the lowest you have scored so far. This is fine, there are no right or wrong answers, providing your answer are true and accurate.

Tactics
This is a fairly small area and only a few factors will actually be influenced by the commitment you have to achieving your goals. While you could skip ahead and quickly read part four to get an idea, here are some examples; are you able to follow a strict taper into your event or will you need to work, be with family or deviate at all? Will you be able to spend enough money on the necessary equipment, bike fitting and other expertise? Will you be able to spend enough time developing your position on the bike?

Much like Mentality, you might find yourself being restricted by your circumstances than your actual commitment here. That is ok, just remember that it is better to find out your goals are slightly out of reach now, when you can reset them, than to train for nine months and find out on the day.

A 10 here will indicate someone who can put everything else aside and focus solely on preparation for their event, especially in the last three weeks leading into it. You might also have a high disposable income and a willingness to spend it on latest equipment or professional advice.

A 1 here would indicate someone who will likely struggle to find consistency in the planning of their event, maybe you know you have business travel or a young family which will make being able to set aside a period of time dedicated to your taper problematic. You might also have money constraints or not be able to afford some equipment or professional help.

Please note that an answer closer to one is not a death sentence, it is merely an objective look at what is achievable, when you relate it back to your goals. There is no judgement or elitism here.

Summary
You need to ask yourself how much you will sacrifice to achieve your goals. At the end of the day, unless you are getting paid to ride your bike, you should be free to enjoy life. For example, if you have children you will want to spend quality time with them, such as taking them for days out or playing in the local park. You will need to sacrifice the things that make life enjoyable if you want to achieve your goals at the earliest possible opportunity.

Consider what you are willing to do to win your goal. Perhaps you would be willing to give up drinking alcohol; perhaps you would be prepared to wake up at 5am every morning, or stop seeing your friends. You need to determine how far you would in the pursuit of your goal. My personal aim would be find the correct balance between how much you want to achieve your goals and how much you want to enjoy the journey. This forms a large part of the Truly Personal Coaching methodology.

Some coaches might take the view that they are not coaching effectively if they encourage their clients to deviate from the most direct approach. My response to this would be to consider how many clients go off plan and even give up completely because they lose motivation, and subsequently sight of their goal, when working at this level of intensity.

Do not score yourself on this section.

Recap
How to score this section:

Take an average of each of the answers you have given; add up all your answers and divide by the number of questions.

Anyone scoring 10 is incredibly committed. You will stop at nothing to reach your goals and they might need everything to go your way in order for you to achieve them. You might not enjoy the training, much of the time, but you might see the most direct and effective route to success.

Anyone scoring 7-9 will see significant increases in just how much they enjoy their training journey, albeit at a small sacrifice to their goals. Your goals will be challenging, and you should be very careful to monitor how often you slip off your plan. The danger here will be complacency, if you keep allowing yourself to train or eat in a manner not befitting your best interest, you might not achieve success.

Anyone scoring 4-6 will be very much enjoying the journey and at this point you are focusing solely on completing your goals at a bare minimum. You are sacrificing very little, but, having a great time on the bike. Your main concern here is that your goals aren't challenging enough, and you could struggle with motivation, or quit entirely.

Anyone scoring 3 or less might want to consider simply enjoying the bike. While it is completely fine that you have scored so little, you might not technically be training, but simply riding your bike. You might have the same issues as above and struggle with motivation towards such an easily achievable goal.

1. Note down an answer, 1-10, about how committed you think you can be to each of the headings; Training, Nutrition, Mentality and Tactics.
2. Add up your scores and then divide by 4.
3. Using the scoring table above, identify if there are any necessary adjustments to the goals you have already considered.

Chapter Three
Goal setting

Case study: personalisation approach

Triathlete Natasha Pertwee engaged my help with her cycling because she was losing a lot of ground to her competitors. At the time, the sport was making a change in some of the rules regarding drafting and she wanted to ensure that she was simply capable of meeting her own expectations.

We established some process and end goals; keeping the right distance while maintaining speed and all out on the road. I spent a lot of time with her, finding ways to adapt my own usual coaching approach. With those process and end goals in mind, we saw a marked improvement in her technical ability as well as her confidence. Natasha went on to represent GB at the world triathlon championships placing high. She also finished her first half Ironman in the same year.

Overall goals
Time for some important questions: What do you want to achieve? What is your why? What motivates you to get on the bike and train? These questions shouldn't be too hard to answer—your overall goal or end product is the main reason you have started this journey. Whether it's competing in a local race, aiming to be world champion, raising money for charity or losing a bit of weight, I don't think I've ever met someone who is training for absolutely no reason.

Long Term
When setting your goals, it's important to look at the bigger picture, so start by thinking about your five-year plan. What do you want to achieve over the next five years? Make sure the goals you set are 'SMART' (In this context: Specific, Measurable, Attainable, Relevant and Time-Bound.)

For example, if you're a rising star in the Olympic Track Development Team, your goal might be to 'gain selection to represent my country on the track at the next Olympics'. The goal is specific to the discipline the rider is in, measurable because you can safely say if the rider made it or not, attainable because they are in the development team, relevant to them and time-bound because the date of the event has been set.

An example for a more casual rider might be 'to ride from Land's End to John O'Groats (LEJOG) within five years. This is SMART because it's a specific route, measurable by having a target which is either completed or not, attainable because it is likely that it could be completed with training, relevant to the rider and time-bound by having a time-frame by which to achieve it.

Keeping it real
Ok, you might have just read that and thought "5-year plan, I'm not thinking that far ahead!". That's ok and in reality, you might not need to. You can go year-to-year just enjoying a new challenge. The majority of my clients might have 1-2 years planned out. I do actually ask for what clients would like to do in 8 years' time. The answers usually include sarcasm along the lines of "be alive" …

What you will get for planning farther ahead is a greater sense of commitment and motivation. I simply can't stress just how important these mental factors will play in your training. 50% of your gains will come from you being mentally prepared, having a strategy for keeping committed and motivated is a big part of that.

But, if you're simply not looking to envisage yourself that far in the future, that is fine, no judgement from me!

Picking your goals
Chances are you have already picked an event that ties in with your overall goal. Some people jump straight in and pick the event,

again, this is fine, and you've not really skipped a step, you've simply not consciously considered the questions I asked at the beginning of the chapter. For most, this isn't a mistake, but for some they will get closer to their events and realise it's not the right event for them, or actually they want something completely different. This is more common in novices, particularly people who want to test themselves against others, they might enter a Gran Fondo, only to get closer to the event and realise that criterium racing is more their thing.

You also need to be realistic with your choice. This might not be from a performance perspective; you might actually need to consider outside factors like work and family or the time you have available. If you want to ride an ultra-endurance event, maybe Race Across America (RAAM), you might be disappointed if your family or work aren't supportive enough, or when you find out how expensive a trip that that will cost. It's important not to limit yourself here, but, at the same time be objective about what you want or can achieve.

Maybe you want to prove to yourself you are capable of great physical strength. If you have a moderate amount of training time per week, let's say 8 hours, you've already completed a few UK sportive events, then maybe it's time to test yourself with a big European one, something that takes in a lot of Alpine climbing. If you want to be in a small collective of people you could try something like Everesting, climbing the same elevation as Mount Everest in a single ride.

Medium term
Once you have your five-year plan, you will need to consider your medium-term goals. What do you need to achieve in the next year? Here's where it can go slightly wrong for some people, as they focus on what they want to achieve, rather than what they need to.

Taking our examples from long term, the medium-term goal of riding LEJOG wouldn't be particularly relevant to someone who wants to qualify for the Olympics. Of course, there can be cross-over, but to take a full year training for something non-specific to the five-year plan is a year lost, which can be critical to success.

However, let's focus on our casual rider as an example. Their five-year plan is to ride LEJOG and they can currently ride a 50-mile sportive at an easy club-ride pace. A great goal for the year ahead would be to finish the Ride London 100-mile sportive at the end of July. This in itself is a SMART objective and a good stepping-stone on the way to their bigger, overall goal.

Once your one-year goal is in place you can break it down into even smaller more specific process goals. These are the individual steps which will help you progress towards those overall goals. Ideally, each component of fitness should have at least one process goal, each tailored to the demands of your target event(s).

Unfortunately, most people who self-train will miss out process goals. Let's again use our casual rider as an example and show some of the process goals which they'll need to achieve this year between now and their target event which, for the purpose of this example, is Ride London.

COMPONENT OF FITNESS	TARGET	TO BE ACHIEVED BY
Flexibility (can also include bike fit here)	To be comfortable riding six hours (100 miles) on the bike	Target event
Aerobic endurance	To be capable of riding 100 miles in one event	Target event

Group riding technique	To be able to move safely around a group of riders in a mass participation event	End of meso-cycle (keep reading for an explanation on this)
Hill climbing ability & technique	To be able to correctly and efficiently climb a hill similar to that of the event	End of 'base' phase

Your plan can have a number of process goals, but it's still worth breaking down the demands of the event and ticking them off when you reach the desired level.

Once you have defined the areas you need to improve, you can break them down into even smaller goals which you can align to a specific meso-cycle. As mentioned in the chart above, this represents a phase of athletic training with a duration of about 4 weeks (keep reading for more information on this).

An example of this would first of all to be 'comfortable riding the bike for two hours with four months to go until Ride London' and then later, 'to be comfortable riding the bike for four hours with two months to go until Ride London' and so on.

You can then prioritise them in order of your weaknesses. For example, if you really struggle on hills, you might make this a priority. Later we will go through how to incorporate this into your training plan.

A rider may be capable of achieving their process goals well before the targeted event and at different rates of improvement. For example, for most, group-riding technique can be achieved in a faster timescale than aerobic endurance. Peaking performance is the exception here, whilst it is great to have a rider performing at 100%, peaking too far ahead of the event may cause a drop off at exactly the wrong time.

Armed with a list of smaller process goals, you'll know exactly what you have to achieve and when you have to achieve them by in order to successfully reach the main target within your plan.

Macro-cycle

An Annual Training Plan (ATP) is basically a macro cycle, which can be a seasonal, annual or a longer-term cycle of training, and it sets out the big picture of your training plan. It might not contain all your goals if you're planning many seasons in advance but should contain everything you want to accomplish in the upcoming year or season.

The idea of having a big picture is to show you exactly what each phase or block of training will, or needs, to achieve. This overview allows you to see progression in a variety of ways as determined by your target events, the time you have available and the way you are training.

For example, you might spend the winter or your base period progressing duration and then dropping this to focus more on intensity as you move into the build phase. It will depend on how much time you have available as to what system you decide to use. Follow this approach, and you'll be able to see exactly what component of fitness you'll target in each phase, and these are explained in detail later. You'll also need to have a specific target or goal for each component and perhaps this might be to increase leg speed by 10 RPM, or FTP by 20 watts.

Again, it will depend on time, but you might factor in your strengths and weaknesses too. Typically, you'd spend the base period (which might be during the winter months) working on your weaknesses and then progress this to working on your strengths the closer you get to your main event. You might even only work your strengths when competing, but mostly this will come in during the build phase (the phase prior to your main events).

The big picture will plot out your targeted events—which are covered in detail a little later on—but it's key that you have included your A events into the plan as a priority so that you can focus your ATP and macro-cycle towards them. B events will be on the plan too and your C events can be added along the way as they may not impact the longer-term plan.

You will also show 'logical points'—usually once per meso-cycle—for such as testing your fitness or performance, tailored to the component of fitness you are training towards. An example using leg speed might be the maximum point at which you can spin your legs without upper body movement or bouncing in the saddle.

Your macro-cycle will also show the rest, recovery and transitional phases, such as an easier week for recovery after a competition phase before starting a new block of training, or a transition between riding time trials and cyclo-cross or just your end of season break. On the next page is a diagram depicting your fitness while following successful macro-cycles.

In chapter 5 *(page 47)*, I will take you through a step-by-step guide to planning your ATP, but, in the diagram on the next page you can see what a season of structured training might look like, if you were to plot a visual line depicting your fitness.

Consider the line tracking upwards as your fitness, with good training and recovery you will become fitter. Unfortunately, the line tracking down is all too common. Poor recovery, over training or any number of other factors, might see your fitness plummet as you are overcome with fatigue.

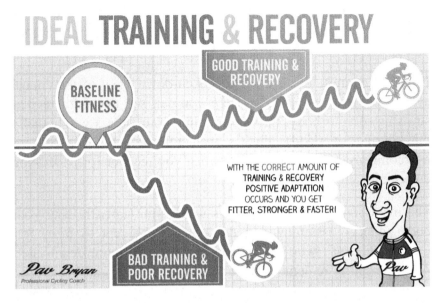

Meso-cycle

A macro-cycle is then broken down into smaller meso-cycles. I've suggested that they might typically take up four weeks, but in reality, they can be any duration, depending on the athlete, the training load, their ability to recover, time spent in the sport and so on.

If you are unfit, new to structured training or suffer with an illness that is affected by training, you might consider a three-week meso-cycle. Two weeks of harder work and stressing your body, followed by one week of easier training, focused on recovery.

A meso-cycle is then broken down into even smaller micro-cycles of about a week long, this again may be affected by other factors, but for convenience seven days would be a typical length.

Plan properly, and you'll be able to understand exactly what each meso-cycle is going to be targeting. You will also be able to see more detail on how this will look in terms of progression over the micro-cycle. A typical example will look like three weeks of progressing duration or intensity followed by a fourth easier week to allow for necessary recovery and adaptation. You might put the testing at the end of the easier week.

In the diagram below, we see a broken-down view of the annual cycle I demonstrated above. Here you can see that with regular stressing of your body, through training, your fitness will actually dip (during overload), this is then followed by a period of overcompensation, or adaptation when you recover (provided you do actually allow some recovery time!).

The main competition icon shows where you start stressing your body again – assuming you don't have an event to taper for. Confused? Don't worry, this gets explained in more detail later. All you need to remember right now is that each meso-cycle is an opportunity to build another level of fitness. Given enough training stress accompanied with enough recovery time, you will see an increase in fitness. Over a period of meso-cycles chained together, much like the Ideal Training and Recovery diagram above, you will see prolonged improvements.

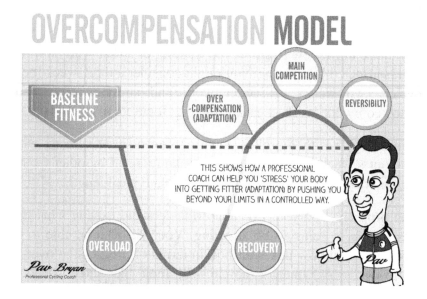

Micro-cycle

About a week long, the micro-cycle will show all of your individual sessions and training. Each session should have a goal with a specific component of fitness, and you could even use the time to work other factors such as technique, tactics, nutrition and so on.

It will also show your measurable key performance indicators (KPIs), such as sleep quantity and quality, resting heart rate (RHR), heart rate variability (HRV), and calorie intake, so you can analyse your performance in detail. If you use TrainingPeaks and other apps such as MyFitnessPal[vi], they can work in sync to save you typing everything out repeatedly.

Much like the meso-cycle, the micro-cycle is an opportunity to see improvements in your fitness. Every day you can stress your body in a way that forces it to strengthen. During each micro-cycle you should have adequate recovery sessions, or rest days, to allow your body to recover from this. The improvements you make on a day-to-day basis might be small, but when you chain together 3-4 micro-cycles into a meso-cycle you see a marked increase in fitness.

Like I mentioned before, when you then chain more meso-cycles together into a macro-cycle, that is where you can really visualise huge improvements. When you think about it in this manner, it becomes really easy to see just how important each session might actually be!

Recap

Using your list of answers to the commitment questions in the previous chapter as a reference, work your way through these points:

1. Ask yourself: What do you want to achieve? What is your why? What motivates you to get on the bike and train? Write this down

2. From this, write down what that looks like over a long term (greater than one year) plan.

3. Once you have your long-term plan, decide on what medium term (approximately one year) goals, try not to focus on events just yet, we will move onto those in the next chapter. The medium-term goals should be specific to your long-term goal and progress you towards it.

4. Identify the areas, or components of fitness, you will need to train in order to reach your medium-term goals, these will form your smaller and shorter-term goals.

Chapter Four
Event targeting

A events

Your A event is the main goal towards which you will be working. Whether you are aiming to win a race or just complete a ride, this is the thing you want the most! In order to achieve it to the best of your ability, you'll need to be in peak physical condition. As such, this is the event you will do the longest, or most effective, taper into. More on tapering in chapter 23 *(page 185)*.

As a coach, I encourage a client to decide on their A events or A goals as early on as possible, and I discourage them from changing their mind about a target event within too short a timeframe. As you will find out, a lot of preparation goes into creating an ATP set by A events and having the events specified early on in the plan is crucial to getting the timing of training and pacing correct. In most cases, a coach has written an Annual Training Plan during a client's end of season break and has timed every micro-cycle to enable peak condition. Changing a client's ATP happens all the time, but it's not ideal close to an A event! In the next chapter I will show you how to create your ATP, but, before you even get started, you should be dead set on exactly what A events you want to do.

As mentioned above, the earlier you know your A events or A goals the better. A event goals don't have to be single events, for example, multiple events would form part of the overall goal of winning Best All Rounder in a regional or national time trial association, combining the average speed across a variety of distances. They could be qualification events for a bigger goal, for example, racing a Gran Fondo to qualify for the Amateur World Championships. In these examples, both events would be A events. Try to set your A events, or at least have an idea of them, during your off-season break. Often, you'll have an idea of what you want to do the following year during the course of the season you're already in, perhaps you can also see the logical progression. Maybe you already know what the next step will be towards achieving your five-year plan. For example, perhaps, in the case of our casual rider, the year after completing Ride London, their target might be a longer or multiple-day event. Setting sights on London to Paris could be the perfect next goal towards the even bigger challenge, LEJOG.

You will set your process goals specifically for the demands of your A events and your training will be designed for them. You might have a considerable taper into these. Tapering will be covered later but you will want to be 100% for these events.

B events

Once you know and have planned in your A events, you can move onto B events. These are the events that you'll want to do well at but will sacrifice being 100% ready for in order to achieve your A events. A good example of this might be a club championship if you are at a regional level. You want to do well but it isn't necessarily your ultimate goal.

B events still need to be planned with reasonable time to fit them in, but only because they might affect training for your A events. There might be a small taper or easy session leading into these events, but you wouldn't stop training to taper into these in a massive way. Although it might seem frustrating to not be at your best for B events, you need to focus on the bigger picture, because B events are not your main target.

C events

Your C events are pretty much everything else. These events can be club time trials, small races used for training, charity rides, club events or something along those lines.

C events could be used solely for training and/or for fun. There is usually no need for a taper or easy session before these, although there might be one depending on the structure of your week.

Your C events are the best time for you to try out something new: that piece of kit, new energy bar or pacing strategy, for example. Perhaps it's on the same course as one of your more serious events. Whilst the result of these events shouldn't matter, you shouldn't waste the opportunity to get something beneficial from the experience. Most C events should offer an opportunity that you should be looking to maximise.

Keeping it real
If you are new to competing, and often when you've been doing it for years, you are going to have some races or events when you are disappointed by your performance. Like being the jack of all trades and never being great at anything, you don't want to fall into the trap where you are trying to excel in each event you do. You have an opportunity to put in some incredible performances, but only if you prepare right and allow your performance to peak through a taper.

Why can't you always or more often be tapering? Because the art of tapering is removing all fatigue from the body to bring up the fitness levels. Do this too many times or for too long and you have reversibility, as it sounds, when your fitness actually goes backwards.

If you are someone who hates to lose, or doesn't like underperforming this is great. There is a big place for your ego in training and competing. It will keep you going when it's really hard and the thought of what others will think or say about your performance will make you dig very deep! However, your ego is also destroying your chance for success.

To be prepared for your A event, you need some practice events prior. These will be the ones where you might want issues to occur, so you can have a strategy for dealing with them in the main event. You might need to get race fit or get used to the physicality of the peloton. You might want to objectify areas you need to improve or test your performance. It's ok to be poor at these events and you should focus on the bigger picture here.

Demands of the event
Once you've defined your A events, you can research the demands that will be required of you. This is often the area that determines just how successful you'll be in your target event and is the area that stops people from reaching their full potential. What you really need to think about here is what your body will need to do in order for you to successfully complete this event.

To demonstrate what I mean, let's use an example target event of a century ride or sportive that takes place across hilly terrain with a large amount on small open roads or lanes. Let's say there's a few thousand meters of climbing in total, with three feed stops and around 5,000 other participants. You will need to define the demands of the event in order to work out what you will need to do to ensure that, by the time the event takes place, you will have the potential to cope with everything that is required of you.

First of all, what sort of duration are you expecting to be in the saddle? If you've not done the event before, you can look to other riders of similar ability—perhaps friends or club members who have completed the event already. You could check their results to gauge what ballpark you could be looking at. Other ways to estimate this include your own previous experience of a similar ride or a test ride. In this example let's say your target is six hours.

So now you will know the first demand of your event—that you'll need to be able to ride for six hours saddle time. There are a few areas you'll need to work on to achieve this which could form process goals. These will be aerobic endurance (simply having the fitness to ride this long), flexibility (being able to hold the position), core strength (applying even power for the duration), and mental attributes such as determination and willpower to overcome suffering.

Your second event demand is the distance and the speed needed to cover the distance in your target time. In this instance, rather than focusing solely on time, you'll want to factor in speed. Using our example, we know that you'll have to average 16.67 miles per hour in order to achieve your target of 100 miles in under six hours.

First, you've got the obvious fitness factor—you'll need to produce enough power to get to that speed and then hold it for the duration. The other factors that'll affect this will be resistance, in the form of wind or rolling, which can be dealt with by concentrating on holding a more aerodynamic position, adding tri-bars, removing parts of the bike, upgrading the bike, clothing and other equipment. Rolling resistance comes down to tyres, where you have the option of substituting greater rolling speed for durability, or in other words, how fast you want to go versus the risk of a puncture. Gravity plays the final part in the equation so the focus here could be to drop weight from either yourself or your bike, this will be more relevant the more elevation you have to climb.

Elevation is a key factor in our example. First of all, you'll need to be able to produce the power required to climb the hills, which we will look at in a bit more detail below. Technically though, you'll need to have the right climbing ability (I see so many riders lose a lot of time by having poor climbing technique, such as gearing and position). Finally, you will need to have strong mental willpower. Again, as with technique, I see far too many riders allowing a hill to mentally defeat them.

Using the example of our target event, you want to test yourself with climbing. Can you mentally achieve it, and have you got the right technique?

What other technical demands will you need to consider? There are many, but let's use our example event and start with group riding. We know that there are 5,000 other participants so ensuring that you can ride safely and change position in a group is a must. Knowing that a lot of the route is on small roads and lanes shows us you will also need cornering, braking and bike handling skills. Next, we'll consider the technical aspect of fuelling. There are only three feed stops in the ride lasting around six hours, so you will need to be comfortable eating on the bike. Riding no handed is a great skill that helps with this, it'll also help with changing clothing—something the weather might force us to do frequently. Of course, you can stop to achieve these things, but when time is a factor, you'll want to minimise this.

Another demand is pedalling efficiency, which can be tricky to identify unless you have a decent dual-sided power meter. Maximising every pedal stroke will be another important factor in success when time is limited. Alongside pedalling efficiency, another performance-based metric is your power to weight ratio. In our example event, there is unlikely to be much information readily available for average power achieved for the event itself. However, you can drill down into individual climbs. We didn't specify each climb in the example, but you could do so. Let's say, for example, you have five main climbs accounting for the majority of time either gained or, more importantly, lost. What sort of power will you need to attain in order to climb them efficiently? In our example, power to weight ratio will be more crucial, as power alone can fluctuate massively from a 50kg to a 100kg rider, whereas time taken to climb may not.

You can look at common power metrics for these climbs (Strava has data available[vii]), or you could do a test climb, have a look at the power output and time and then logically calculate what improvements in that power output you'll need to achieve in order to get to the top of the climb in the desired time.

Next, we'll consider the demand of nutrition. In our example, what would be your prime energy source? With only three stops and with a reasonably strict time-frame, you won't want to stop too long and will need to carry some food with you. Some of the fuel will be from your body's own stores but knowing that it'll potentially be a slog up some of the climbs and, primarily, your body will be using carbohydrate as fuel means that food will need to be consumed outside of stops.

With this information to hand, you now know that you will have to experiment with different fuelling sources to establish whether gels, bars or drinks will be palatable and sit in well in your stomach. Go to the necessary lengths to find out what food is available at the feed stops in order to test this out. Bear in mind that feed stops might not be the most hygienic places to get food. You will not want to risk having a bad stomach, so the stops might be used solely to just fill up your water bottles.

Hydration is also a very important consideration. You will need to know how many bottles you'll need to drink in order to complete the sportive. In most circumstances you'll carry two bottles on the bike and stop to top-up, which can form part of your stopping and pacing strategy. What goes in the bottle is also important, you will need to consider whether you should take your own energy sachets or hydration tablets to add to fresh water rather than relying on what's at the stops.

The last event demand I feel worthy of mentioning is tactics. You should consider getting a good warm-up. The last thing anyone wants is an early injury, so planning a short period at the start to focus both the mind and body will reduce that risk.

Understanding the tactic of pacing is key to your success. Using a power meter to pace the climbs will be fairly easy if you have already done testing and understand what output you can achieve over what duration. If you're not measuring power, heart rate information can also be used. Without either of these, you're left with your rate of perceived exertion, how your body feels and the question 'can I sustain this effort for the time required?'

In the case of our sportive example, you could get into a group which will dramatically increase average speed. A timing prompt taped to the top tube can also be useful, it will tell you, for example, that you need to be at a feed stop by a certain time. Not only is this a good visual prompt but a good back up should something happen to your bike computer.

With the knowledge of what the event demands, you can then set process goals with some specific tests, based on the weaknesses you have identified, to ensure you achieve success. For example, if you need to improve core strength then you might consider Yoga. Then a progress test might be how long you can hold a plank for. In this manner you can really quantify improvements.

Recap
1. Taking the goals, you have set in the previous chapter, identify some (1-3) main events you want to target.
2. Using these main events, identify smaller events you could use as training or to test performance.
3. Also note down any other events you will do.
4. Armed with your list of events, research and then note down exactly what the demands are for each one. What will you need to be capable of to be successful?

Chapter Five
ATP

Nowadays, thanks to training portals such as TrainingPeaks, you can consider your Annual Training Plan (ATP) as an outline training programme[viii]. It might cover a year or a season, but it's the foundation for where to start. For most people, it will be seasonal with a natural break, but this is not absolutely necessary.

This is the big picture of your approach to your cycling training, outlining each stage leading up to your key event of the year. Typically, your ATP is split into four blocks: base phase (or preparation), build phase (or pre-competition), race (or competition) phase and transition (or recovery). Then repeat next year / season.

Each phase has specific targets, designed to help you build up towards achieving your overall goals. For example, if you're training for a long ride in the summer, you might focus the winter months on building up your base endurance and working on your core and flexibility. That way you will know you have the capability to at least sit on a bike for the duration of your event! After that, your training programme might look at improving your velocity or how well you climb.

A word of caution; the ATP outline is a great guide, but it's not a tablet of stone. Whether you have a change of mind or something happens that's out of your control, such as injury, you can adjust it accordingly. Likewise, you can do so if you feel you have been under or over ambitious.

Here is where your first major decision will lie. What approach will you take to building your ATP? A traditional periodisation model will have you riding a lot of slow and steady miles during your off-season or 'base' phase. Typically, this is winter, that time of year where riding a lot of slow and steady miles is less than appealing. Once you have successfully built enough time in the saddle, you will then be ready to start adding some intensity to that and making it more specific as you move into the 'build' phase of training.

A reverse periodisation model does exactly what the name suggests; swaps the training around. In this method you would train intensity during the winter, this is music to many people's ears, no more drawn out steady, and wet, outdoors rides. Then when the sun comes out, you'll be ready to start riding outdoors and getting the miles in.

Both of these common systems have their flaws, some more obvious than others and it depends on what your targets are. Here is what I'd recommend you start by doing, it is a simple system that works with a lot of people and if you are new to structured training, this will be a logical place to start.

After you've set your goals, the first question you should ask yourself is "how many hours per week do I have to train?". Once you know this, you're going to have a pretty good idea of what your 'base' period will look like. Almost all of the clients I work with have less than 12 hours per week. The majority actually around 8 or less, with many 5 or even less than that! If you have 12 hours or less, you're probably not going to get much from doing a typical 'base' phase where you go on a lot of low intensity, steady rides. In reality you might need 20 hours plus to get the most from this sort of training.

The training methodology is suggest is making your training more specific, the closer you get to your main events. For example, you want to ride 100-mile event in summer, then your training should get closer to that goal as you approach the actual date. You want to target a 10-mile TT, then as you get closer to your event you should be spending more time at that intensity, for the duration you want to achieve. This might fall under either a typical periodisation or reverse periodisation approach, but it might also mix parts of each.

With that in mind, here's what I recommend you do: After each 'recovery' phase, where you have taken a short period of time, one to two weeks perhaps (depending on how busy your previous season was) off the bike, you should start with a short 'preparation' phase. This will be super easy riding, maybe all indoors where you can monitor it and make sure you don't go too hard, you might focus on leg speed (cadence). You might also add some light gym work, exercises you might do from home and body weight only, where you focus on form, with slow reps, no weight. You might also incorporate a stretching routine, or something like yoga or Pilates.

This phase will strengthen your tendons, ligaments and increase flexibility. In short this is the phase that reintroduces the idea of training to your body. Getting this phase wrong, or skipping it entirely, might increase the risk of injury and decrease the likelihood of you being able to sustain performance improvements throughout a long off-season of training.

You might spend one week in this phase for every half a week you had off the bike. For a single week 'end of season' break you would spend two weeks prepping your body. For two weeks off, you would spend four weeks in prep. It is unlikely you will need more than four weeks to prepare your body. You should be feeling energised and motivated throughout this period, it should not be taxing, and it might be a little boring. That is ok, you'll thank me later!

Once you have moved on past this phase, you will need to do some 'base' work. The good news is you don't have to do longer slower rides. Training at a higher, yet still aerobic, intensity reaps very similar rewards as longer, less intense training. Since you don't have time for the latter, make the most of the former. Depending on how many weeks you have until your event, you might spend one more phase doing simple sessions at a higher aerobic intensity, we will look at zones in chapter 7 *(page 64)*. During this phase you will also continue to work on your leg speed (cadence), this will become crucial later on in the training, read on to find out why.

Once you have completed this phase you are ready to start laying some strength groundwork. The off the bike work you have been doing will now include some heavier weight work with less reps. Don't worry, gym membership is optional, if you can afford a home gym this is advantageous, but you can improvise with other heavy objects.

You might also introduce some on the bike strength work too. Low cadence efforts, starting with some simple accelerations and building to longer intervals. The idea of this phase is to increase the maximum load your muscles can sustain. This will make power improvements all the easier in the future phases.

Power is derived from the amount of torque you can produce; consider this your strength, multiplied by velocity, or the speed at which you can spin your legs, remember me mentioning you train at high cadence. You can of course, have a lot of torque with low leg speed or vice versa to achieve the same result, so, don't worry too much if your body simply can't handle much leg speed or you are more of a spinner.

But the above formula is exactly why you should conduct this training before smashing the super intense work, you will simply get more from periodizing in this manner.

Now what you have got to remember is to make it more specific to your goals the closer you get too them. Your body will also reluctantly train both for increased power and increased duration, some people can handle this, but, focusing on one at a time might reap greater rewards. This might mean that, for someone riding a century, you only have a small period to build that power before looking to more sustain it while you build saddle time.

If you have previous data to look at, examples of how your body will cope with specific training, what your strengths and weaknesses are, you will have a far easier time planning your ATP. As a side note on strengths and weaknesses, you might consider spending a lot of your off-season time strengthening your weaknesses, so that when it comes to getting specific all you have left to do is strengthening your strengths. If you're wondering why, simply consider the last time you left something big to do too late to get right.

With the online training portals, it is no longer necessary to rewrite your ATP from scratch when you need to make changes to your key targets. However, while the annual plan can change, having it completed at the start is a critical tool for success and a huge motivator for when the going gets tough.

Whether you are considering things on a day-to-day level or visualising the year ahead, your ATP provides context for every piece of the puzzle. When you can see the bigger picture, you can see how all the pieces fit together and how crucial each one is to your success. In this respect, I do recommend using TrainingPeaks to manage your ATP alongside your coach because you can see exactly what you've done and what you still need to do.

Let's take a more detailed look at each individual phase. While there are a few ideas about how long you should spend in each phase, I will not outline them here. When building your ATP, work backwards and allot an amount of time you think you will need for each phase, this should be an objective assessment of what you think you will need to do to reach your goals and what your strengths and weaknesses are.

Base phase
Could also be called general or preparation phase, this is the period when you're not specifically training for an event, and where you might do some training that doesn't replicate your A race. For example, with non-specific or base training, you might work more on your weaknesses. You might go for long steady rides or keep the intensity up if time isn't on your side.

However, whilst base training is non-specific, be aware that it still needs to serve a purpose; there's very little point in five one-hour turbo sessions in zone one, see chapter 7 *(page 64)* for an explanation on zones, spread throughout the week since you will get minimal adaptation from this.

In all training, what we are looking for is an adaptation. Simply put, you stress your body by doing the training; it might be easier to think about lifting weights here. Once you rest and recover, your body will strengthen the systems you have stressed, in our weight lifting example this might primarily be your muscles. This process is called adaptation and you will hear this term a lot throughout your training, from your friends and in this manual.

Many people will continue with intense work throughout their off-season, and whilst this can certainly help, you need to be very strong-minded for year-round specific work and there is a risk of suffering from burn-out long before the season starts.

While there are a few definitions of burn-out, it is a term that I use for mental fatigue. Your body might be fine and coping, but your mind might be suffering. This is increasingly common among those susceptible to depression, including seasonal based, chronic and even other mental health challenges.

A better option might be for you to use cross-training as a non-cycling workout to build strength, with swimming being a great cross-training activity. Alternatively, you could use an intense gym-based programme such as CrossFit, and I'd add here that adaptation is the key to building strength and mental agility.

Following the system, I outlined above is a great place to start if you are a beginner to structured training. As you accumulate more knowledge and data on yourself, you will be able to make smarter choices about how best to spend, arguably, the most important time of year for cyclists.

You might be reading this wondering how you would make all this work, perhaps your strengths are power and you're training for a century ride. Maybe you don't want to spend the winter riding outdoors or you don't have time to put those hours in. Everything can get a little confusing. Here is my advice on the order of priority, during this phase, that you focus on achieving. This will help if some training falls in more than one category:

1. Weaknesses – 100% train what you are weakest at in the base phase, sorry if that also means you need to start building saddle time now!
2. Time availability – if you only have 5 hours per week then training low intensity won't do much good. The only exception is when this is a weakness.
3. Personal choice – if you're not enjoying the training now, you'll probably be fed up of it by the time the event you're looking to do arrives. Do yourself a favour and pick training you will enjoy! However, if you have certain weaknesses and a time availability issue, you have to make a call, either find a way to enjoy it, suck it up and do it, or find a different goal.
4. History of mental health – if you've had challenges in the past you should be looking to factor that in here. Ask

yourself, and be honest (or ask a close family member or friend), whether the ATP you are setting yourself will be too taxing on your mental health.

5. Event specific and strengths – these are the least important during this phase. Unless of course, they also fall into one of the above categories.

You might be able to think of a few more that are specific to you, just be objective in how you deal with them and slot them in within this list.

Build phase

Also referred to as the pre-competition phase, this is commonly where you take all of the work you've done in the base phase and turn it into more specific training that is tailored to your forthcoming events. In the traditional periodisation model, you might be dropping the overall duration of your training session, but increasing the intensity. It is, of course, dependent upon your time availability and your goals!

If you are following my sample system or have been training with limited time all year, this might be where you actually start to do more riding. Hopefully this times well with the weather turning more pleasant. I can hear your cheers in the back of my head!

In this phase you might also be strengthening your strengths. Here are my priorities for the build phase:

1. Event specific – training should be getting a lot like your event or goal, the closer you get to it.
2. Strengths – strengthen those strengths, but not at the cost of any training that is event specific.
3. Weaknesses, time availability, personal choice and history of mental health all come in here, for the same reasons as base and in the same order.

Competition phase
This is what you've been training for. Here, you're not necessarily looking to make training gains, but to sustain them. Typically, there will be limited training as you compete in the target events at whichever level your goal was. During this phase, the aim is to keep fresh, recovered and ready to race.

One of the biggest mistakes I see is athletes trying to have a competition phase that is too long. Take World Tour professional cyclists, the longest they look to be in peak physical condition might be three weeks. You might not be a world tour athlete; therefore, you might consider having less than three weeks at peak fitness before starting training again.

This is where it is important to try to split up your A events. Too many, too close together might mean that some you suffer for. Ideally, they need to be split far enough about for you to have a very short transitional and base period, before then another build and competition phase.

Recovery phase
As you move away from competition phase, you need a focused recovery (or transition) phase. Typically, this will come at the end of the cycling season and you may take a complete break from the bike. If you're aiming to peak more than once during the season, you might use this period to relax and enjoy riding without training, allowing full recovery before you start a shorter period to rebuild into a further competition phase in the ATP.

Lots of mistakes are made here. Typically, this is eagerness on the part of the individual. Having just finished an A event and wanting to get preparing for the next. Regardless of what time of year your recovery phase, be that end of season or just after a key event, ask yourself this questions "if I had to take a week easy, would I prefer to do this right after one of my A events or right before another?", I think we are unanimous in answering this.

A word about FTP

One of the key components of training is Functional Threshold Power (FTP) and you may want to build estimations of the maximum power that you can hold for one hour into your ATP targets. This is especially true if you choose to use a system built around FTP, like TrainingPeaks.

This FTP system was first espoused in an academic paper, Determinants of endurance in well-trained cyclists, in 1985 and introduced the idea of how to train and race with power[ix]. It's different for everyone, but once you know your FTP or MMP (Maximum Minute Power—set by testing such as incremental ramp or three-minute test—you can establish your training zones, see chapter 7 *(page 64))*.

I don't specifically ask my clients to use power meters, but many coaches do. These meters used to be expensive, but if you have the budget, they do help you to understand and have confidence in your pacing, with the information you need on hand at a glance.

Recap

1. Start by plotting your events into a calendar. You can use a paper-based system, but, TrainingPeaks ATP is excellent for this.
2. Working backwards plot each phase of training. We will come onto tapering later, if you know your ideal taper plot this in, if you are new to tapering then start with 2-3 weeks. This period will come directly before your competition phase, where your A events are.
3. Once you have planned each phase, probably 4-week cycles, identify what component of fitness you will train, or focus on, in each phase. Remember to reference your weaknesses and my list of priorities to ensure you have every aspect of training plotted into your ATP.

4. Plot your easier weeks into the phases, be careful though as you might not want an easier week at the end of a phase that precedes your taper, you're simply adding another week to it!

Chapter Six
Progression

You now have your goals, what you need to do in order to achieve them and your overall plan in the form of an ATP. What next? Well here is where it starts to get fun, let's look at progression in terms of training[x].

First, are you going to have your end of season break and then go straight back in at the same intensity as you were just before it? Probably not. Why? Well for a start, you've just had time off the bike, without prepping your body you are increasing injury risk and leaving your body fighting to recover from such efforts. With that being said though, how would you structure progression into your training plan?

The demands of an event, that list you created in a previous chapter, will dictate the order in which to progress your components of fitness, but commonly, endurance is trained in off-season and maintained through to racing with the higher end work such as sprinting, anaerobic and short-term muscular endurance being the main focus closer to your target events.

If you have been following the advice in the previous chapters, you now have your list prioritised and tailored to what you need. Don't blindly follow anyone else's plan at this point. All you need to do is work out how to progress from where you are, to where you need to be.

Reversibility
Most athletes most hated word! Don't worry, some is natural, and at some point during your year you will experience it. Like I mentioned earlier though, it is better to take a week off at the end of one season before starting preparation for the next than to need to take it nearer to your event.

The good news is the body is commonly thought to 'remember' training[xi]. The longer it takes to train a component of fitness, the longer it takes to lose it. In other words, since it takes a considerable amount of time to see adaptation from steady state low intensity work, it will take considerable time to see reversibility or detraining of this.

This is fairly easy to test. Take two weeks off the bike, say at the end of the season, and make a note of what, in terms of power output, you lose first. I showed you my training pyramid in chapter one. The power at the top of the pyramid, your maximum output, will go first, then it trickles down.

Age
Certain circumstances might dictate intensity. For example, the older you get the harder or slower it is to build the top end, so maintaining it might be crucial throughout your off-season[xii]. In this instance, there is little point leaving threshold work until 8-12 weeks before your event as valuable gains are unlikely in this time.

You'll start to figure it out for yourself in no time, but consider what your targets are. If you are aiming for a century ride, you don't really need to be maintaining sprint power all year round. You don't even need to train it, really! But it's a nice change and can bring around some other adaptations. For the century ride, you might consider keeping some intensity throughout the year so you're not starting from scratch. This might still be aerobic, around FTP and you may even push a little over that from time to time. Anything that'll simulate hill climbing would be good, unless you are planning on doing a flat century!

To get the progression right, think about building your power first. This might look like shorter intervals with plenty of active recovery time. We are aiming to get your power output higher and then, once you're satisfied your power is where it needs to be or you have to move on due to timing with your ATP, move onto sustaining that power for a longer duration. This might still be intervals, but rather than pushing your limit, in terms of increasing power, you are pushing your limits as you look to hold that power longer.

Don't make the mistake of going out and trying to do both at once. Make it easier on your body, build that power, then look to sustain it for longer.

Time
Time will play a big factor in what you do to progress. If you're time-strapped, then training all at a lower intensity might not provide your body with enough adaptation to make it worthwhile. Therefore, you might want to spend your precious time at a higher intensity to make it more beneficial.

Again, take a look at the demands of your event. This will tell you exactly where you need to train. Much like if age is against you, look to build power first, then look to sustain it for longer. That is where the progression lies.

Anaerobic and sprint power
In order to reduce the risk of peaking early and fatiguing, top end power threshold work is usually saved for the last 8-12 weeks before A events, but there are exceptions where this may not be possible, feasible or valuable, some of which I mentioned above.

You might also move between different levels of racing throughout the year, spending summer racing on the road, then spending the winter doing cyclo-cross. However, this makes the typical way of leaving time to progress your top end power work more problematic.

Overall, it's important to ensure that you factor in your main targets, the time it will take you to reach your required outputs and the journey needed along the way. You will also need to decide the component of fitness you will need to train in a given phase, and then ensure you can progress it.

If one of your weaknesses was top end power, then racing throughout the winter might not be a bad idea. You could focus on track competition; this is a great way to build that sprint and explosive power. It might be advisable to not take up all of your time, but, be a focus point within other training, like finishing a club ride with an all-out sprint or doing the weekly club chain gang. You might be focusing all of your training time on this sole component of fitness, but you are ensuring that you are on course toward your targets.

Much like the previous examples I provided, you will be looking to increase maximal power at any given marker, for example peak/sprint or VO2 max, they are different, but you'll follow the same principles of progression I mentioned.

Aerobic power
If you are following my ATP example and focusing on upper aerobic endurance work during the winter, you will be looking to build up your power output, this might be your FTP, and eventually you will switch to sustaining that longer.

Once you have completed your power work, you will then move onto training to ride longer (you will look to maintain power during this phase of training).

I recommend hours over miles as you can't control the weather, or some terrain might be different each ride. For example, if you have one person who lives in a flat area and another in the mountains, who will be out riding a century ride the longest?

Then logically progress the amount of saddle duration towards the demands of your target event (this might simply be the duration you plan to ride your event in).

If you have identified this area as a weakness, it might take you a long time to get to your target, especially if you are new to the sport. However, if you find that you have a good base, you could achieve your target duration very quickly. Then you could look to build power sustained within that duration. Again, it's worth me pointing out that rarely does it serve you well to try to improve power and duration at the same time. Give your body a chance!

Pitfalls

The worst thing you can do for progression is to go too hard too soon and then not be able to improve over a training cycle thanks to fatiguing early and needing a break. Think about the logical form of progression and take into account your event. This is especially important the closer you get to it. If you do use the winter months to build a steady base, then progression might look like hours you put in rather than intensity. Provided you have the time, this might be the most beneficial to you. If you don't have the time to effectively progress training in this manner, then manipulating intensity might be the only option you'll have for progression. Reducing recovery time so you spend more time at a higher intensity is an option.

Progression is to no avail without adequate recovery. Without allowing your body the time it needs to recover and adapt from the training; you'll eventually burn out and suffer fatigue. If you continue to train on top of inadequate recovery, you could start to get sick, suffer injuries or even get chronic fatigue syndrome. In order to avoid excess fatigue, you will need to consider which you prefer: an easier week to recover after a hard block of training or several weeks, perhaps right before your key events or in the height of summer, of less strenuous but more sustained training.

Be sure

Test at each step! It's very simple to devise a test to ensure that you are progressing a specific component of fitness. In a previous example, I suggested testing leg speed by the ability to hit new maximum revolutions per minute before any upper body movement or bouncing in the saddle occurs. FTP, MMP, CP (and the rest!) are done by their own relevant tests, see chapter 7 *(page 64)*. To test core flexibility, hold a plank. To test strength, you could use one rep max squat weight. Just work out where you need to be, and this usually provides the method to test it.

Recap

1. Using your list of prioritised components of fitness, plot out your progression in each. Here's a simple example for climbing a certain hill:
   a. First you might to train to be able to 300 watts.
   b. Then you might to be able to hold 300 watts for 10 minutes.
2. Do you have any factor which might affect your progression?
3. Plot regular testing throughout your ATP, make it relevant to the component of fitness you are targeting for each phase. Easier weeks are great for testing, aim to make testing repeatable.

Chapter Seven
Monitoring

No matter what aspect of training you are focusing on, you will need to have a method by which to monitor it. Training with power is currently very popular and it is becoming increasingly more affordable. The vast majority of my clients use power meters and it's likely there will come a time where it'll be more common than not to see a power meter on a bike when sold.

There might also be times when training 'blind' is useful. In most cases, whilst it can be liberating, training blind limits the opportunity to see progression and improvement. Going out for a non-training ride is great for mental freshness, relaxation and for not constantly obsessing about what your power output should be. But perhaps the Garmin in your back-pocket approach is the way to go so you still have a record of it! While 'if it's not on Strava it didn't happen' isn't at all accurate, if you don't have a record of it, you might also regret that!

Try to use as many monitoring methods as possible. The most common three are power, heart rate, and rate of perceived exertion, which we'll explore below.

Power
With the price of power meters coming down and more companies entering the market, there has never been a better or more affordable time to join those who have been using a power meter to monitor their training, fitness, fatigue and pacing in races. As a coach, it does make my job of monitoring, reviewing and prescribing training a lot easier and more accurate. If you can afford a power meter it can be one of the biggest ways to improve your training, but you'll need to learn how to use it effectively!

There are good blogs and articles out there about power meters and there are many opinions on the subject. In my opinion, what's important is learning how to use a power meter effectively so that you can quickly get the most from owning one without being too bogged down in the detail.[xiii]

Here are my tips to help you get setup with a power meter. First of all, set up your Garmin / Wahoo (or another device) correctly. I'd recommend turning the smart recording setting off. The other setting you need to consider is 'zeros', or more accurately whether your average power includes or excludes the times when you're not producing power and/or cadence. I can see both sides of the argument but one thing we probably all agree on is that once you decide whether or not to exclude down time, stick with it, don't chop and change as this will affect the data over a longer timeframe.

Your screen needs to show you relevant data. I'm not a fan of using current power as it fluctuates too much. Instead, consider using three second, thirty second and total average. This will show you the power produced at any given time, over a period of time (reflecting a harder or easier effort such as a climb or descent) and also the total for the whole ride. Alongside power, you should still have other useful data in front of you, for example, cadence, distance, time and anything else you feel relevant.

You should also make use of other screens. If you are going to be doing some interval training, then having a screen setup to show you laps, lap power, lap duration and other relevant metrics, will be crucial. You might also consider having a screen for leisure rides versus training, the former having less data on it just so you don't get carried away.

Ensure you set to zero or calibrate your power meter at the start of every ride (refer to manufacturer handbook on how to do this), as this will ensure that you get a realistic reflection of power output, although outside temperature changes can fluctuate power readings.

You shouldn't simply rely on power data alone. A 300-watt effort may feel easy on one day and almost impossible on another. Your heart rate and perceived effort will tell you a lot about how your body is dealing with producing any given power output. You shouldn't be alarmed if you sometimes struggle—it might be expected based on, for example, the conditions or timing of your training or racing (unless of course you're expecting it to be easy!).

With this in mind, it becomes crucial to know your route (course if racing) and the expected conditions, and equally important to pace yourself correctly. As with other aspects of training, pacing is an area where you can get various answers from different people. I feel it's always better to go slightly harder uphill or into a headwind knowing that you can recover slightly going back down the hill or with a tailwind when it might be hard to keep your power up anyway. One other thing to remember when pacing a race; although you might have a best power output over a given distance it will change depending on terrain, don't just expect to be able to always hit the same power outputs on different courses, have a power personal best for each course as a guide.

With a power meter you have an accurate method to test progression and improvement from training.

You may have heard of an FTP test, see chapter 7 *(page 64)*. Functional Threshold Power is a good way of monitoring progression over a period of time, but there are also shorter tests, some as short as several seconds, which may be more relevant to you depending on what your targets are. You can still get an accurate a reading of fitness from these as you would a 20-minute FTP test without the extended time in protocol.

Don't get too hung up on solely improving FTP, there are also great gains to be had by spending time on improving your position, techniques, tactics and other areas. Above all, it is prudent to include a variety of testing in your training to ensure that you are improving across a variety of areas.

Monitoring software such as TrainingPeaks has made viewing your data simple and you can easily visualise improvements over time using indicators such as TSS (Training Stress Score)[xiv]. Whilst these are valuable tools, I'm sure nobody rides a bike simply for the numbers and, equally, I'm not a coach who relies solely on data, but it helps me to do my job as effectively as possible.

Heart rate

If you don't have a power meter (and even if you do) heart rate is a valuable tool. There are very few athletes nowadays who don't use heart rate information in their training. Heart rate monitors are relatively cheap to buy, very easy to install and simple to use.

Sadly, the biggest problem is that heart rate is easy to influence. Anything from a poor night sleep to caffeine intake can have an impact. These many contributing factors make effective and accurate monitoring of training and racing harder.

Another problem is just how easy it is to misread your heart rate. If you don't know what you're doing, it can become incredibly difficult to understand and account for the changes and fluctuations in heart rate. I've met with a number of athletes who have told me they are getting much fitter because their heart rate is lower but within days are suffering with sickness or poor form.

Much like power data, heart rate needs to be used in conjunction with how an athlete is feeling. Your heart rate may be lower but if you are feeling unwell this could be a sign of fatigue. If, however, you feel great then you can conclude that you are getting fitter whether or not you have lowered your heart rate.

For this reason, if you're training to heart rate alone it becomes incredibly important to keep accurate and relevant notes alongside your training. Reviewing how you were feeling at any given point during a certain training period is impossible if you don't log your ongoing training experience (see section on training diaries coming up).

Rate of perceived exertion

How you are feeling during times of exertion is crucial to understanding what is happening in your body and there are a number of easy methods to monitor this. I use a simple 1-10 scale, where 1 is so easy you could do it all day long and 10 is so hard you can only do it briefly before feeling like you want to throw up!

The Borg scale is another method, which uses instead 1-20 (sometimes starting at 6). I prefer 1-10 as I think you get enough information from this scale.[xv]

It's also important for you to learn how to judge how you are feeling. Power and heart rate data is only reliable when the meters are giving accurate readings, failure to calibrate correctly can lead to considerably variable and unreliable data on your screen. Knowing how you should be feeling at any given point in training and racing can be a reliable pacing tool.

You might also fall back on RPE throughout your time training. Here's an example, you have trained a long winter and can now do a 10-minute effort at 300 watts with a heart rate that is 10 beats per minute lower. Are you fitter or more fatigued? Well the answer could actually be either. If you can do that effort and feel comfortable, good and fresh then you are arguably fitter. If you do the effort and you feel terrible, like you are having to push through with all your willpower, you might actually be more fatigued. Heart rate can both be lower if you are fitter or more fatigued, the crucial difference here is how the effort felt.

Analysis

Once you have your data, you can start to analyse it for useful insights. Perhaps you're looking at what went well in a race so you can replicate it in future—you may, for example, see that you were more effective at implementing your pacing strategy. Maybe previously you were burning too many matches and not able to hold the power at the end.

Comparing data from two similar sessions, tests or races is a good way to monitor progress. Improvements in fitness can be seen, for example, through more power output for the same heart rate or the same power with a lower heart rate. You can also record and analyse your tests. For example, a leg speed test at the start and the end of a training block taking into consideration factors such as heart rate, power and cadence to ensure that physiologically the training has had a positive effect and you're not just spinning your legs faster and hoping for the best!

One of the key points for me is how a client feels while riding. Testing has some limitations, a perfect example being the difficulty to conduct an FTP test in heightened heat. You can, of course, tailor the testing to this problem but something to ask yourself is do you feel better riding? Albeit subjective, that's the main reason why some amateur cyclists train. What's the point in spending hours in pain if you can't enjoy cycling at some point?

Analyse whether your training has actually made you a faster cyclist. Consider the following three factors affecting your cycling performance; rolling resistance (weight/gravity), power and air resistance. There's always the potential for cyclists to lose weight to increase performance, but too much of the wrong type of weight loss results in power loss too (and if you're suffering with malnourishment and fatigue, you're almost certainly not going to be faster).

The same goes for increasing your power. Perhaps you've over-eaten and now aren't as aerodynamic or just plain heavier. In both the above examples you've had a negative effect on your power to weight ratio (watts per kilogram of bodyweight).

Your analysis will show these symptoms but only if you know what to look for. Blindly following just one measure, for example, power or weight, is a recipe for disaster as you'll lose focus on the rest. Analyse all key performance indicators.

One thing I recommend you avoid is comparing yourself with your friends or other athletes. However, understanding the general requirements needed to achieve your goal can be gained through comparison. For example, I've spent years building a database of comparable data through testing and open resources. From this I know what Maximum Minute Power output is needed to be able to be successful in entry level road racing, or what power to weight ratio you need to be a hill climb specialist.

When using comparison for analysis, don't blindly compare figures with your best mate, you are likely to be two people with a different set of circumstances. Instead, look at an average across a far wider audience or someone who is very similar to you.

The best piece of advice I can give for improving your understanding of data analysis is to read through the help pages of the tracking software you use. I use TrainingPeaks and there's a wealth of videos and blogs that help to better understand how to use their system to the greatest advantage.

Training diaries
As mentioned previously, one of the most effective tools for monitoring your progress is to keep a diary. There are lots of different tools you can use including paper-based records, spreadsheets, TrainingPeaks, Today's Plan[xvi], Golden Cheater[xvii], Strava and many more. Keep a record of everything you've done so you can look back and figure out what worked and what didn't.

What information should you keep a track of? In addition to the data we have discussed, make a note of how you felt before, during and after a session, what worked, what could be improved and anything else you feel is relevant. Be aware of the quality of your notes, it is no good just uploading or writing down the time and distance of a session as you'll look back and have no idea how you were feeling or if you did something different or special that day that may have influenced the outcome.

Include other information such as key performance indicators; resting heart rate or heart rate variability, some of which are covered previously. With time, patterns may occur that you wouldn't normally notice. This can be very true in particular with nutrition and weight.

In almost all cases if you miss or skip a session it's not worth playing catch-up. If you have a coach, this is where they become invaluable as it removes any bias from your decision. If you self-coach, then you need to make a decision about what the main goal of the block of training is and what that individual session is giving you. If you are looking to build FTP over a four-week block, then skipping the easier session to catch up on a harder one might be correct. Having said that, you also need to factor in recovery to the next session. Will completing this session out of the original order mean you're not recovered for the next key one?

It's worth noting that when amending your training calendar, TrainingPeaks doesn't save a record of what you'd originally planned, therefore, you might want to make a note about how you changed it. My clients simply make notes about the session itself and I then make ongoing necessary adjustments to the original outline plan.

Alongside working with my clients' training diaries, I use social media to add motivation. I have a private client Facebook[xviii] group where I make weekly announcements on who has done a particularly good race or test. I also make a 'green week' announcement to acknowledge who has completed all the sessions as prescribed and therefore turned the session green in TrainingPeaks.

For you, if you don't have a coach, motivation could come from involving friends or family on your journey. Share with them your aspirations, what you need to achieve and check in with them on each step. This will go a long way to keeping you accountable and increasing your motivation (see chapter 17).

Monitoring via testing

The most common way to set your training zones is to use a standard measure of testing such as Maximum Minute Power or Maximum Heart Rate (MMP/MHR), Functional Threshold Power or Heart Rate (FTP/HR) or Critical Power (CP)[xix].

MMP/MHR can be tested by taking the average power from either the last 60 seconds of a 'ramp test', in which you incrementally increase power output until failure, or by taking the average power across a three-minute all-out effort. The latter could be conducted using a hill climb and could form the basis of a maximum heart rate test. Once you have your maximal levels you can set your zones accordingly.

FTP/HR can be tested in a variety of ways but the most common is a 20-minute sustained effort taking 95% of the average power achieved. This is an approximation of the power you can sustain for one hour based on the 20-minute test, from which you can set your zones. If you use TrainingPeaks it will be very important to test this regularly to ensure that your dashboard and TSS is correct, even if you don't use FTP to set your zones.

I prefer Maximum Minute Power (MMP), simply because I think that the shorter duration test is easier to complete. It's over very quickly and even when you're having a bad day it's often comparable to previous scores, where as a Functional Threshold Power (FTP) test may vary wildly or sometimes feel impossible to complete. You can find alternatives to test progress and almost all tests can be used to find an approximation of other values, for example MMP can be used to estimate FTP (just take 70% of MMP to get FTP).

Once you have set your zones you should still look to monitor improvements across a range of key performance indicators. For example, to check the strength of your core a relevant test would be to see how long you can hold a plank, then to do 3-4 weeks of core training before retesting. If you are targeting a sprint, then do a sprint test, such as six seconds all-out effort. You could do a variety of adaptations from standing still to rolling at a certain speed. You could use Strava to set a time for you to beat within a certain segment. A hill climb is another perfect example of a relevant test—whether you are aiming to be a National Hill Climb Champion, or you're just targeting a sportive and struggling with hills.

Training zones
In order to maximise gains through training you might train using zones. Training zones are specific percentages of your functional threshold power (FTP), functional threshold heart rate (FTHR), maximum minute power (MMP) or maximum heart rate (MHR), which you can determine via testing. The most effective way would be to set your zones by power, however, if you are lacking a power meter, you will have to use heart rate.

Once you've established your training zones, you're ready to train in them! For best results when using zones, you might train indoors where you can fully track your progress during your session and ensure that you remain within the zones you've decided to train in. However, you can still train outside using zones if you have a suitable environment; made easy by not having interruptions such as traffic lights. You shouldn't totally replace outdoor training with indoor; with careful monitoring you can get the best of both. It's worth noting that you might factor in outside training rides into your plan, with flexible zonal shifts and fluctuations.

Recovery rides should almost always be done inside because the only way to ensure you stay in the recovery zone is to train in an environment that you can fully control. If you go outside, you should be riding so slow that old folk are riding by you!

Zones 1 and 2 are easily achieved outdoors on long club rides where saddle time takes priority over intensity. For these two zones, I wouldn't recommend spending long hours indoors and once you get past a certain duration, zones become less important due to fatigue. Just getting long steady rides done is what zone 1 and 2 are about.

The remaining zones (3-7) are achievable in both environments depending on what your goals are. For purely monitoring purposes, indoors might always be better, but there are a number of considerations beyond this, such as the mental aspect of training. I'd always factor in conditions when setting a client's programme; an interval session can be done outside on a beautiful, hot day. The athlete will enjoy it more and be more inclined to follow the plan. Sometimes training outdoors can provide a technical boost opportunity too, in particular sprint training in supra-maximal zone, the most intense. It's also worth mentioning that some forms of cycling might always benefit from being outdoors' specifically those that have unconventional positions, such as time trial or ultra-endurance.

On the following page are two tables that break down each zone, including the parameters, importance of the zone and what adaptations you are looking for. Ensuring you get a good mix of each zone is important to boost your overall cycling ability. Factor in the time you have available and always consider the session's goals. For example, what will a one-hour zone 1 ride achieve? Is it not worth using that time a little better?

Training Zone	Purpose	% MHR	%MMP	RPE (1-10)/How you feel	Duration
Recovery	Regeneration and Recovery	< 60	< 35	1 Very relaxed. Able to carry on a conversation.	< 60'
1. Basic	Establish base endurance	60-65	35-45	2 Relaxed. Able to carry on a conversation.	90'-360'
2.Basic	Improve efficiency	65-75	45-55	3 Working. Feel warmer. Heart rate and respiration up. May sweat.	60'-240'
3.Intensive	Improve sustainable power	75-82	55-65	5 Hard work. Heart rate and respiration up. Carbon dioxide build-up. Sweating. Breathing hard.	45'-120'
4.Intensive	Push threshold up	82-89	65-75	6 Stressed. Panting. Sweating freely.	30'-60'
5.Maximal	Sustain a high percentage of maximal aerobic power	89-94	75-85	7 Very stressed. Gasping. Sweating heavily.	14'-40'
6.Maximal	Increase maximum power output	> 94	85-100	10 heavily stressed. Gasping. Sweating heavily.	4'-10' intervals
Supra-maximal	Increase sprint power output	N/A	> 100	10 extremely stressful. Gasping. Sweating heavily.	Short intervals

Training Zone	Purpose	Physiological Adaptations	Race fitness
Recovery	Regeneration and recovery	Increase blood flow to muscles to flush out waste products and provide nutrients	Promotes recovery and therefore training response
Zone 1	Establish base endurance	Improves fat metabolism, gets muscles/tendons/ligaments/nerves used to cycling. Increases economy	More efficient use of energy. Prepares body for harder training, works on technique/skill
Zone 2	Improve efficiency	Improves the ability to use oxygen, produce power and increases efficiency	Able to produce more power with the same level of effort, works on technique/skill
Zone 3	Improve sustainable power	Improves carbohydrate metabolism, changes some fast twitch muscle to slow-twitch	Improved sustainable power, good for all cycling events
Zone 4	Push threshold up	Improves carbohydrate metabolism, develops lactate threshold, changes some fast twitch muscle to slow-twitch	Improved sustainable race pace, useful during tapering or pre-competition periods; too much time in this zone can cause staleness
Zone 5	Sustain a high percentage of maximal aerobic power	Develops cardiovascular system and VO2max, improves anaerobic energy production and speeds turnover of waste products	Improved time trialling ability and resistance to short-term fatigue
Zone 6	Increase maximum power output		
Supra-maximal	Increase sprint power output	Increases maximum muscle power, develops neural control of pedalling at specific cadence	Develop race-specific skills at race pace, starting power, sprint speed, and the ability to jump away from the bunch

If you are using TrainingPeaks, you might actually consider leaving training in zones behind and going more specific with %FTP/HR. With TrainingPeaks workout builder[xx], you can structure each individual session with an exact power, heart rate and cadence goal. This makes training very easy and to add even more user-friendliness you can export these sessions to Garmin devices, Zwift[xxi], TrainerRoad[xxii], Sufferfest[xxiii] and many other platforms.

Recap

1. Choose your method of monitoring; power, heart rate, rate of perceived exertion or as many as possible.
2. Choose your method of analysis and where you will keep your diary/notes (non exhaustive list): TrainingPeaks, Today's Plan, Golden Cheater, Strava or any other.
3. Choose how you will train: will it be zones set to MMP/FTP or as a specific % of MMP/FTP?
4. Set a baseline in whatever method you choose. Remember you might need to adapt this depending on the component of fitness you are training (go back to your prioritised list of training needs here).

Chapter Eight
Recovery

All your hard work in training is nothing without the adequate opportunity for recovery and adaptation. Recovery is fundamental; some people say that without it you're over-training, but I prefer the term under-recovering[xxiv].

When you finish your session or race what do you do? Usually, you have a golden window of about 30-45 minutes in which you can help your body kick-start the recovery process. During this time, you should be focused on returning your body to a state equal, or as close as possible to your pre-training state. This includes heartrate, body temperature, glycogen and hydration levels. I would suggest that this be achieved by spinning your legs out for at least 10 minutes, preferably using a turbo or rollers. Aim for light gearing and low power with a high cadence. This should help flush your legs, reduce your heart rate and start to settle your mind and body.

Once you've spun your legs, next up is stretching. (For instructional videos subscribe to my YouTube channel[xxv]) Stretching will help to keep your legs from locking up later and can reduce muscle soreness.

You can also look to reduce or increase body temperature to a normal state. Ice baths are a tradition among many professional sports people and there are even portable systems which can help reduce the temperature of your body and specific muscle groups in order to promote recovery. If you've raced in a cold environment, you need to get layers on immediately even if you don't feel cold. This allows your body to focus on recovery and not having to keep warm. If you're wet, you'll also need to get dry quickly, so I'd suggest that you always pack a towel in your kit bag even during the summer months.

Next up, a tip that is more a preventative measure than promotion of recovery, I'd recommend that you treat the period immediately after racing and training as though everyone around you has some horrible contagious illness. Your body's immune system will have been weakened by the training and you are therefore at heightened risk of catching something. Pay particular attention to cleanliness, hygiene and others around you during the recovery process.

Replenishing lost fluids and carbohydrates is also key for good recovery. You can test how much you sweat fairly easily by weighing yourself before and after a session. You can just as easily check the colour of your urine after training or racing, the darker the colour the more dehydrated you are. Drink sensibly until your urine is almost clear and note that, outside of training, the most important time to check the colour of your urine is first thing in the morning. Just because your urine is clearer during the day doesn't mean you are hydrated; water might be simply passing through you.

Working out how much energy you've expended isn't as easy as most trackers make it look, but as a guide they are better than nothing. Depending on how well you've fuelled during your ride, when it comes to replenishing carbohydrate you'll be tempted to reach for the nearest sugary, fatty piece of junk you can lay your hands on, but approach this with caution. Although you'll likely be at the best point to eat these types of food from the perspective of not putting on weight, you're not going to do your recovery any favours by eating rubbish. To really boost recovery, you need an optimal amount of carbohydrates, mixed with good quality protein.

I am a big fan of getting a meal in straight after a session. Real food beats any form of man-made or processed supplement or addition to your diet. Think 'food first'. In many cases either this won't be practical, or the idea of a meal will make you feel queasy, in which case a recovery drink is a close second.

My advice for a recovery drink is to make your own, it's easily achieved. For carbohydrates add a mix of fruit such as a banana and 80-100 grams of strawberries, or other fruit, with about 25 grams of quality oats. Protein is a little harder to get into a shake so having a ready-made powder might be useful. If you're not a fan of this idea, then try adding seeds or nuts, which'll also add fat to the macro-nutrient replenishment too.

Something to be aware of here; while replenishing fuel is important post ride, you might consider how you are fuelling and what diet you are on (see more in chapter 12). If you have an adequate protein intake throughout the day, you might not need to hit that protein shake immediately after training – your body has enough, and it knows what to do with it.

How you continue to replenish expended energy after the initial period will greatly depend on what you're doing with your training and goals, and thus nutrition. Periodizing your nutrition to match your training will greatly dictate how you eat. Periodized nutrition is how I would describe changing the ratio of carbs/fat/protein that you consume depending on what sort of training you are doing. A perfect example would be if you are training at low intensity, either with the goal of building steady base fitness and promoting your body's ability to burn fat as a fuel source, increasing the amount of fat you consume as a percentage of your overall intake might aid this. Similarly, when you are racing or doing a lot of high intensity training eating a higher percentage of carbs might be more beneficial. You can train your body to run more efficiently on fat too, armed with this you can run your body on its all but unlimited stores of fat at almost any intensity.

Your recovery will be optimised by carefully considering your ongoing daily nutrition in addition to the window immediately after training. If you consider the carbohydrates, protein and fats (macros) as the fuel you put in to your car, then the nutrients you get from plant (micros) will be the oil that makes it run smoothly.

You can put the most expensive fuel in a Ferrari but if you don't put any oil in to the engine, it will seize up! What micro-nutrition does is help your body repair the damage done to your cells through exercise and many other factors such as poor air quality or toxins in our food and drink.

Consider increasing your daily intake of fresh food. Really focus on what you are eating and why you are eating it; ask yourself if the next thing you eat will add further to your recovery time or reduce it, this will motivate you to make smarter eating choices.

I'm a big fan of eating little and often, neither grazing nor eating massive meals but thinking about getting your daily requirements from 5-6 meals of approximately 500 calories each, adjusting this depending on your training load. Meals should be made up of good quality carbohydrate, protein and fats. Experiment with the ratio of each as this can be very individual, and consider your periodisation of training and nutrition. As mentioned previously, you could consider eating more fats when your training is at a lower intensity and more carbohydrates when your training is harder.

You should always have your optimum recovery in the back of your mind. In addition to good food, sleep is vital, and although rarely practical, getting a nap in after training or racing can be the biggest boost to your recovery. If sleep isn't an option, then try to elevate your legs or reduce the amount of time using them.

Massage is excellent for muscle recovery and, in addition (or instead of if you aren't able to have regular massages), make the foam roller your best friend. Although horrible, it is an amazing way to promote recovery and the one bit of kit I'd recommend every person should have and use regularly. Again, subscribe to my YouTube channel for instructional videos.

Think about where recovery gains can be made in your day-to-day life. For example, take the lift rather than the stairs, take adequate rest and minimise the amount of work your body has to do outside of actually adapting to the hard work you put in during training.

Using the rule of asking yourself whether you are adding or reducing the time needed to recover when going about your daily life will open your eyes to how much more you can do to aid recovery. Despite work, family and life getting in the way, consider even the smallest margins as the difference between winning or losing a race or setting a new PB.

KPIs
Looking at Key Performance Indicators, or metrics, on a daily basis can tell you how fit or fatigued you are, and can go a long way to understanding whether you're doing too much or too little.

The following KPIs are an excellent measure of recovery and will indicate how well you are recovering. They include resting heart rate, heart rate variability, mood, energy levels, sleep quantity, sleep quality, diet, medicine taken, muscle soreness, weight and training load (list non-exhaustive). In life, there are many factors affecting how we're doing on a day-to-day basis, too many to list, but these are the key aspects that you'll want to be aware of, since they impact every other area of recovery when they are out of kilter.

First of all, with regard to energy levels, how do you feel when you wake up? It's simply not healthy to wake up every day feeling groggy, tired, lethargic, and as though everything is a struggle. If this sounds like you, then there are many possible reasons, but first consider whether it could be one of the following three things: a) you could be training too much and not allowing yourself enough time for recover; b) it could be your diet, either because you're not eating enough or not enough of the right foods; c) you could have a medical condition. Spend some serious thought on the first two, because more often than not it's one of these.

While it's perfectly normal not to jump straight out of bed upon waking, getting up in the morning shouldn't feel like climbing Mount Everest. You'll also need to factor in the air temperature upon waking as no one likes getting out of bed when it's cold.

Next, consider how much sleep you have had and whether it was of good quality. Below is an extract from an article in RCUK[xxvi] to which I contributed.

Sleep is the body's way of shutting down, so that it can recharge and recuperate for the following day. Without sleep, the body is unable to function at all. For cyclists, the key and most measurable benefit of sleep is the physical effects it has.
During deep sleep the body repairs all the damage you've done throughout the day and through training. Without sleep the hard work you do on the bike will not produce the adaptations you require, meaning your body will not adapt and become better at dealing with the training stress you are putting it under.

Inadequate sleep doesn't just mean you'll stay still and not make progress, but in fact could potentially move you backwards as your body (and mind) becomes overloaded. As a result, your immune system can become compromised, and muscles and tendons more susceptible to pulls, strains and tears, as well as the risk of burnout increasing, too.

If doing exercise is catabolic and breaks down your body's muscle tissue, then your recovery is when your body is able to be in an anabolic state – where muscle tissue is able to rebuild, adapt and grow stronger to the demands it's being put under. Recovery after training is key to enable you to do whatever it is you're doing, more easily with less effort in the future.

In a nut shell, sleep is where this benefit is maximised. It's when all the hard work you've done in training has its effect. Your body is able to repair without distraction: blood vessels, muscle damage, as well as hormone regulation are all addressed when you sleep.

It's also crucial for mental health and general wellbeing. Think about when you've had a bad night sleep; you feel tired, lethargic, with a lack of alertness and awareness for the next day. This is your brain trying to function without adequate sleep, and the same is happening to the rest of your body.
With a good night's sleep your body will adapt and recover quicker. One of the best—albeit least practical—recovery methods from hard training is a quick nap after, allowing your body and mind to reset for the rest of the day.

While it is possible to perform surprisingly well on a reduced amount of sleep in isolation, the cumulative effect of a lack of rest and recovery will soon have a negative effect. It's also dangerous. Lack of sleep can leave a person lacking alertness. On the road, where you need to be ready to react to objects in the road and changing road conditions, that can be a recipe for disaster, for you and your fellow road users.

In short, someone who gets enough sleep every night will be able to perform better. They will recover quicker between training and will be able to train harder, faster and longer, for repeated days. Additionally, they will potentially get sick less because their immune system will function better.

Training load, as well as other contributing factors such as work pressures and your personal life, also have an influence on this requirement. If you're particularly busy or stressed, this taxes your mind and body more, so your sleep requirement will naturally increase, alongside the increased need for sleep and time to recover due to physical activity.

You can try to compensate ahead of a race or major ride and 'build up' sleep, so that if you do have a compromised night before the big day, the after effects aren't as bad. Certainly, this has application for long sportives, where the start time can be as early as 7am, and an alarm call much earlier to rise, eat breakfast and get ready.

Left to its own devices—with no alarms to interrupt sleep—the body will settle into a regular and natural sleeping pattern. The NHS has most recently published guidelines of between 6-9 hours per night for an adult. For some this can generally be as little as six hours, and for others as much as nine. If you're finding that you regularly sleep for longer than nine hours and are still feeling tired, it could be time to visit the doctor. Finding the root cause could reveal other underlying health problems.

Of course, getting 'enough' sleep isn't just a case of counting the hours. The quality of sleep is absolutely vital, too. There are a multitude of things which can negatively affect sleep, including stress, diet and lifestyle, and these can potentially cause insomnia or, at the very least, disrupt the quality of sleep and your body's ability to truly shutdown.

There are also a number of simple things you can take to improve the quality of sleep and one key step is to remove yourself from artificial light before going to bed. You should aim to either turn off all sources of artificial light, or have a rule about not checking IT devises after a certain time, giving your mind time to switch off from the stimuli. I also advise trying not to fall asleep with the TV on, because the light and noise will disrupt how deeply you sleep even if it doesn't wake you.

Sleeping conditions are also important and that includes factors such as the quality of your bed, temperature, humidity, general light source, as well as smells and pollution. In fact, most experts suggest that making the bedroom a dedicated space for sleep, devoid of distractions, is one of the best ways for creating an atmosphere conducive to sleep.

Additionally, eating and drinking immediately before bed can lead to disrupted sleep because your digestive system is working hard. In particular, you should avoid things with high caffeine and sugar content, which will spike your blood sugar and put a hold on your sleep. You should also avoid over-hydrating, because getting up repeatedly in the middle of the night will disturb your natural sleep cycle.

Ensuring you relax before trying to sleep is also important. For example, breathing exercises might work particularly well if you've had a particularly stressful day. The more relaxed you can be before you go to bed, the better the night's sleep will be[xxvii].

Thirdly, consider the quality of your diet. As mentioned previously, diet can play a massive role in understanding other indicators. A poor diet will affect your sleep, weight, body fat, recovery and energy. Once you learn how to effectively monitor all these factors, it will become obvious how influential your dietary habits actually are on your overall health and, naturally, the knock-on affect this will have on your recovery and performance.

Next, make a mental note of how much muscle soreness you have. It's common to hurt more the day after a heavyweight session than you will after a standard training ride, but if you're sore all the time, consider your energy levels, sleep quality, or diet as possible causes.

Next, your weight and body fat percentage, along with changes in either of these, can be another indicator of how you're doing. Subtle changes are expected as part of a bigger cause, for example, weight loss will be gradual over a long period of time as will bulking up a bit to produce more power. What we are looking out for is sharp and inconsistent changes in either (or both) weight and body fat that could reflect either empty glycogen stores (could be a difference of ½ to 1 kg) and/or dehydration (could see drops of even more).

When monitoring body fat percentage, it's important to try to pick a method that is accurate. Bathroom scales are notoriously inaccurate but should show consistent information and therefore can be used to track changes even if they might not reflect the true value.

Finally, consider external stressors alongside how hard your training has been. This plays a key part in a good understanding of all the other contributing factors. If you have been training very hard, perhaps at the end of an overloaded week, it will be understandable to be showing red flags across some of the other KPIs, but if you're just ticking along normally and have no reason to show these signs then perhaps it is an indicator of ill health.

RHR

For some years, Resting Heart Rate has been a gold standard measurement of fitness. The common understanding of 'lower heart rate equals higher fitness' is probably one of the most misunderstood facts in sports science. Of course, you can see trends where people who are fit and healthy have a lower RHR than those who are unhealthy but when you are looking at this from a progress-monitoring perspective it is unlikely that a drop in RHR actually shows that you are becoming fitter, unless, of course, you have started at a fully untrained level.

To make RHR relevant and a useful tool, what you need to do is establish a baseline. The easiest point at which to do this is while you're on an end-of-season break when you should be fully recovered and fresh. Heart rate apps can do a little of this via guesswork and algorithms so there is no need to take a week or so off during the season just to monitor your RHR.

Once you have your baseline it's then just a case of monitoring it. Apps are perfect for the job since they can plot a graph showing trends and you should be able to see what effect your training is having over a specific period of time. The information can also show warning signs of doing too much, for example, a jump in either direction of more than five beats per minute can indicate something outside of the norm. If you can't find a reason for the change then, potentially, it is a warning sign of upcoming illness, but, in most cases, this spike or dip could be attributed to hard training, a poor night's sleep, poor diet; or any of the KPIs we discussed.

In conclusion, RHR can be a tool to help plan your training, and certainly useful over a longer period. However, relying on it solely is difficult and problematic. I prefer the much more in-depth Heart Rate Variability (HRV).

HRV
Your heart beat is not a constant. For example, if your resting heart rate is 60 that doesn't mean that your heart beats once every second. Heart Rate Variability takes into account the difference, not just in BPM of your pulse, but also in its consistency.

A quick one-minute test every morning using one of the apps available on all smart phones followed by some subjective questions will not only add value to the measurement but also help you to understand and listen to your body. Many apps are available, but I recommend HRV4Training[xxviii] as it uses just the camera on a smart phone.

Again, these systems act as a warning against overtraining or sickness, small changes over a longer period of time can be hard to notice so most of the apps have detailed views of all metrics as well as advice based on the pattern of your variability.

The more data you input into these systems, the more accurate your reading becomes.

Listening to your body
Case study
Damen Foord is an aspiring young cyclist who competes in short distance time trials and one of his goals was to qualify for the Amateur World Championships. Damen and I worked closely together for a number of years; taking almost five minutes off his 10-mile TT time. Damen works as a joiner and his job can be physically demanding with some days having to travel long distances to price up jobs. One of the areas that I worked with Damen to improve is his ability to listen to his body. Damen knew he could always come to me for advice, but I left him with the ability to know when he is capable of training and when he needs more recovery. I feel a true gauge of how well a coach works is the ability to ensure that the client learns. With Damen's new ability to listen to his body, he will be able to judge whether training is going to make him feel better or worse without the need for a coach.

You can have all the fancy gadgets in the world, track everything, write everything down and monitor it, but it all means nothing if you don't know how to listen to your body.

There's a fine line between not feeling up to training and not feeling like it. For me the key difference is that the former is your body telling you to recover and the latter is your brain making excuses for you. Whilst you need to ensure that you are not just finding excuses not to train, if you feel absolutely terrible that's a pretty good indicator that you need to rest, recover and be fresher for your next session. If training makes your situation worse and, subsequently, you need longer time to recover; you'll regret it in the long run. Your key weekly sessions should take priority; you should begin to understand how long it'll take you to go from feeling tired to feeling fresh. If you think that completing a session will cause your priority session to suffer; skip it.

There are some key warning signs that indicate some form of fatigue or burnout. There are probably too many to list but, generally, I find that clients will complain of feeling down or depressed. Lethargy, tiredness and lack of sleep are common indicators of fatigue, along with repeatedly picking up sickness and injuries or poor performance in racing or training when expecting good form.

However, if you truly can't face cycling or training, lack motivation and keep thinking of excuses you could be suffering from burnout. Burnout is the mental equivalent of chronic fatigue, which can accumulate over months and take months to get rid of. Asking yourself how you feel and keeping track of it via a diary can show trends. Be aware that sometimes you might expect to feel fatigued, for example, at the end of a hard training block but you should equally expect your recovery to be visible.

Recap
1. Write down your recovery plan based on the information above.
2. Ensure that you have time to implement this all. For the time poor individual, you might need to cherry pick certain aspects, or even consider cutting training time down to focus on more positive recovery techniques.
3. You don't need them, but you could search out the latest recovery tools: compression wear, suits, cryo-suits, electro-stimulants and even oxygen chambers.
4. Download an app like HRV4Training, and start to log every morning.

Chapter Nine
Individual needs

One of the reasons behind pioneering the Truly Personal Coaching method was to put an end to mass generic 1:1 coaching. You will never receive the same plan as your friend (or anyone else) if you pick a coach with whom I work. As a British Cycling Level 3 coach and through my own personal experience, I've been shown the correct way to identify the best way to make coaching work for every individual need, of which there are a great many[xxix]. Here, we look at three of the most common differentiators. If you have an individual need not listed here and would like to understand how you can get training to work for you, please get in touch, it would be great to hear from you.

Age
Your age will make an enormous difference to the way you train and should be approached on a case-by-case basis in tandem with other factors such as time in the sport or general health.

Under 14 years old: generally, I would not consider formal distance-based coaching if you are in this age bracket because the quickest way for you to become disinterested in the sport would be to put you into a training regime. I'd also recommend that if you fall into this age group, you should consider participating in multiple sports and seeking your local British Cycling Go-Ride club who can nurture you as you develop, teach you the right skillset and help you get into racing.

14-16 years old: someone showing great potential in cycling, who is interested in cycling, might start to train with more structure at this age. If you are in this age group, a professional coach might introduce a plan which is enjoyable, will build key components of fitness in a very limited time frame and also, initially, want to factor in additional recovery time for you such as one day on / one day off. This is a great way to ensure that you don't do too much.

16 years and over: at this age if you are dedicated and committed enough you could start to concentrate on just one single sport and really focus on training to win. Recovery will still be an important factor for you, but more stimuli could be introduced to take advantage of your ability to adapt. From this age, school work becomes more focused and, as your body matures, extra care will need to be taken in order to ensure that you have the mental strength needed to proceed with structured training.

30 years and over: depending on the amount of time you've spent in the sport of cycling, being in this age group will tend to be the time when you reach your peak. Maintaining performance becomes crucial. You might weight train all year around to ensure you don't lose muscle mass. You might also reduce volume but keep intensity high, this will increase the amount of time needed to recover without losing any top-end performance. End of season breaks may be shorter, to limit losses.

Gender

There are some key physical characteristics which typically make men and women different. Without focusing on what it is that makes these differences apparent it is crucial that, as a coach, I do not expect everyone to respond to a training programme in the same way, even when I am coaching two similar people of the same gender. What I notice more than anything is the difference in mental characteristics between each gender. Men might often project an independent or macho picture of themselves, but only truly evolve as a cyclist when they allow someone—such as a professional coach— into their way of life. I find it fascinating and truly honouring when someone allows me to get this close to them, it typically reaps much bigger rewards when you can see the true picture of what is happening in someone's life. Women have very little problem accepting that they might need the help of a professional coach, rather than focusing themselves on what makes them great cyclists they want to hear what others have to say on the matter. The encouragement of a coach is crucial to the success of the athlete—especially, but not exclusively, in the case of woman. With either gender, it is very rare to find someone who responds positively to the 'tough love' approach.

Disability

I've worked with a wide range of people with different specific needs due to having a disability. For example, if you have type 1 diabetes, you may need help to understand the role your diet plays when trying to balance blood insulin levels[xxx]. Equally, if you suffer with a mental disability such as Bipolar Disorder you may need more concentrated help to understand the mental attributes that make a successful cyclist. I've never turned a client with a disability away and it saddens me deeply when people approach me having had that happen to them. As a professional coach it is very rare that a person with a disability gets more time with me than those who are able-bodied. Except for at the initial setup and research phase, the disabled person just gets my help in a different way. If you have a disability of any kind, please do contact me about your training needs and, wherever possible, I will try to help in any way I can.

Case study
I have a client with MS who needs weekly injections and, for that day and the majority of the next day, he is unable to train. I then spend a lot of time trying to restrict his load during the remainder of the week as he has a tendency to want to play catch-up with everyone else, I can see his frustration but when he rushes out to do more than he should he easily becomes sick. We work very closely together to ensure that his health comes before his cycling. We look to maximise his training gains through shorter, more intense sessions and really focus on how he recovers. In tailoring his training to his unique circumstances, he continues to see incredible improvements in the sport he loves.

Part One - Recap

If you have followed this part correctly, you will now have:

1. Set yourself some goals, both long and medium term.
2. Identified some target events for the next year.
3. Setup your Annual Training Plan.
4. Identified the training you need to do.
5. Identified any external tools you need to help.
6. Identified your ideal recovery routine.
7. Tailored this to your exact needs.

Congratulations! You are one quarter of the way through this book and, if you implement your plan correctly, 15% closer to achieving your cycling goals!

In all seriousness, despite it reaping the least rewards, from my ratio of where your improvements come from, this is the most technical to do, and somewhat most fundamentally important. At the end of the day, you won't ever reach your cycling goals without doing some training, whereas you might achieve them on poor nutrition (it's not like you can stop eating) nor poor mental health (although you will likely quit if you don't look after this crucial aspect!).

Part Two
Nutrition
'You can't out exercise bad nutrition' (Anon)

Chapter Ten
General understanding

The quickest way to lose any of your hard-earned training gains is to neglect your nutritional needs. Imagine for a moment that you are a car. If macro-nutrition (carbohydrate, protein and fat) is your petrol then micro-nutrition (nutrients and minerals) is your oil. You keep your Ferrari topped up with petrol, but if you forget to put oil in it then the engine will seize up. The same goes for your body[xxxi].

Macro-nutrients
Primarily, your macros are your fuel. Carbohydrate and fats are burned for energy and, to some lesser extent, so too is protein although protein also has a protective role in your body, as does fat. I would not recommend that anyone in training should reduce almost to the point of elimination any one of these groups—the body needs balance.

At low intensity, in most cases, your body will start to burn fat as a fuel first. This will primarily depend on how 'fat adapted' your body is. To put it simply, you can train your body to run more efficiently on fat as a fuel source. As you start to increase the intensity, your body will turn to a more readily available fuel source, carbohydrates.

What this means is that while, at high intensity, carbohydrate will become the primary fuel source, you can make more most of an almost unlimited fuel source, fat. This does require training and, in some cases, simply might not be necessary to your goals. This information is responsible for the increase in athletes switching to nutritional programmes like the Ketogenic diet or HFLC (High Fat, Low Carb). We will look closer at specific nutritional programmes in chapter 12 *(page 106)*.

I'm not an advocate of any one diet or nutritional system. My work with clients and my research into genetic influence on nutrition has taught me that what works for one person, might not for another.

Genetics plays a big role in what diet you should look to follow, as does intolerances and allergies[xxxii]. Athletes with certain genetic markers might be more sensitive to carbohydrates, meaning that they will see a significant spike in insulin levels upon eating them. This can lead to fluctuations in energy and mood, not ideal. Similarly, certain people might have genetic markers which suggest they don't digest saturated fats well, again, this can lead to digestive issues relating to feeling sluggish and fatigued.

What do you do? Well my advice would be to seek out a reputable DNA testing company, we use Fitness Genes at Spokes. This, actually rather affordable and non-invasive test, will give you all the info you need on what diet you are 'genetically' suited to. It will give you a lot of other information that will help your training too.

Armed with this knowledge you will be able to make a decision about your nutritional needs a lot easier. But what if you don't want to do the test or cannot afford it? Well you can simply try a few out, give each nutritional programme at least two weeks and make adequate notes as to how you feel and what your performance is like. Do not follow the advice of your mates, nor follow the advice of anyone biased or trying to sell you a product or service related to that diet. Because, why would the keto diet salesman tell you that carbohydrates are good for you? That's right, he wouldn't because he wants you to buy into his high fat programme!

As we move on, here's a bit of basic information about each of the macro-nutrients.

Carbohydrate

This fuel system is easy to access but the stores are limited. It's simple enough to top back up again, although your body is limited to the amount it can replenish on an hourly basis. Your body will be capable of burning well over 1000 calories per hour during intense exercise. The majority of this might be carbohydrate, but you'll only be able to replenish around 250 calories per hour.

Your body might have a capacity of around 2000 calories from carbohydrate stored as glycogen, so a good guide would be that, whilst training, a rested person who has full stores might last two to three hours before reaching the point at which their body runs out of available glycogen and therefore has to switch to burning fat as a fuel source, thus slowing down considerably. (This state is known in cycling terms as 'bonking'.)

Good sources of carbohydrate were once considered to be white bread, pasta and other highly processed foods. It's up for discussion, of course, but I strongly recommend you try fuelling from cleaner, less processed foods. I'd also recommend avoiding gluten where possible, but I wouldn't recommend blindly using 'gluten free' options—learn to spot the difference between marketing spiel and quality food[xxxiii]. In general, if it comes in a packet, it's probably not the best you could be feeding your body. Potato, oats, rice and starchy vegetables, are some examples of unprocessed produce and are better sources of carbohydrates than that in a packet. Get your faster fixes of energy from fruit; mix it up, eat a variety and enjoy.

One portion equals (the size of your fist)

- 50g jumbo oats
- 50g millet flakes
- 200g sweet potato
- 50g brown rice
- 50g quinoa

- 4 rough oatcakes

Protein

Protein is made up of amino-acids, which form the building block of muscles in your body. Protein isn't typically used for energy but in the absence of carbohydrate or fat your body will turn to protein as a fuel source. In this event, you'd be likely to undo much of your hard work since your body might cannibalise muscle in order to create fuel. But, by ensuring you get a balanced, well thought out diet, you should give yourself the best possible opportunity for continued growth in cycling.

While the ratio between fats and carbohydrates might change between what nutritional programme you are on and what the demands of your event are, once you know what amount of protein your body needs per day, this usually remains constant. This might typically be between 20-30% of calorific intake. If you find yourself frequently getting sick, or have slow recovery you might want to increase your protein intake. If you have skin complaints such as a rash from something you ate, while it's important to remove the irritant first from your diet or life, such as pollen, pet dander or food like dairy or gluten, a lack of protein might be why your body takes a long time to repair the damage to your skin.

More is not always better and too much protein can be problematic. Your body doesn't need to be flooded with protein in order to grow; it just needs the right amount at the right time. As with all of your macros, ask yourself where your protein is coming from—good sources are fresh meats, fish, eggs, legumes and soya (tolerances permitting). Try to buy local and organic, the former being more important than the latter if you have to make a choice. Local isn't just good for your friends and neighbours. Reducing the time it takes from farm to fork will increase quality and taste!

Consider moderation and quality with your meat but don't worry too much about the fat content in some meats, saturated fats are not the issue we once were told they were[xxxiv]. However, limiting your intake of saturated fats from meat products might make you healthier. Clean and lean will always win; chicken, turkey, fish, eggs, grains like quinoa, and legumes such as kidney beans. For anyone looking to eat less or no meat, plant sourced protein is readily available in the shape of produce such as soya, quinoa and legumes. Pea, hemp and seed powders are also good.

One portion equals (the size of your palm):
- 150g chicken or turkey breast
- 125g tinned tuna in spring water
- 125g lean red meat
- 150g cooked beans
- 150g cooked lentils
- 2 large free-range eggs

Fat
Fats are essential to good health. They won't necessarily make you fat, but the type of fat you eat will determine how healthy your diet is. Schools of thought change with research, but current thinking is that hydrogenated trans fats—the synthetic fats found in processed foods—should be avoided completely and saturated fats found in meat products should be eaten only in moderation or even better, replaced with saturated fats from plants, such as coconut[xxxv].

On the other hand, unsaturated fats promote healthy joints, brain function and cell growth. As with protein, unsaturated fats, will also help you to feel fuller, so if you are looking to restrict calories (although if you're reading this you might not be) then eating a meal high in unsaturated fats and protein should stop you reaching for snacks later. Good sources of unsaturated fats include olive oil, avocado, oily fish, egg, seeds and nuts. It's also worth mentioning that very dark chocolate or cacao, although not naturally high in unsaturated fats, in moderation counts as a healthy food.

Need an easy to remember way to determine between saturated and unsaturated fats? Saturated fats are solid at room temperature, whereas, unsaturated fats are not.

One portion equals:
- 1 tbsp. of olive, pumpkin or sesame oil
- ½ medium avocado
- 20g flax, sunflower, pumpkin or chia
- 20g (2 squares) 70-85% dark chocolate
- 50g hummus

Calorie Counting
What is your goal? If you are trying to lose weight you might want to consider calorie counting. I'm of a mixed opinion with this. There are some people who this really works for. There are others that it doesn't. Ask yourself these questions to see if calorie counting is a good idea for you:

1. Are you looking to maintain or add weight?
2. Are you concerned, anxious or worried about your weight?
3. If you have counted calories before, have you ever spent more than a week in calorie deficit?
4. If you have counted calories before, have you consistently tried to be in more than 500 calories deficit in any one day?
5. Have you ever suffered with fatigue, tiredness, lethargy or a similar condition for more than two days consecutively?
6. Have you ever suffered with depression, low mood, irritability, stress or a similar condition for more than two days consecutively?
7. Are you training a lot, either in volume or intensity, or are you within four-six weeks of your target event?
8. Are you currently suffering with slow recovery, in comparison to what you are used too?

If you answer yes to _any_ of these, I'd strongly recommend you do not calorie count and you just eat listening to your body. There is no need to eat until you are stuffed. If you ever start to feel ravenously hungry, this is your bodies way of telling you that you are not eating enough. When you start to feel this way, it is a matter of time until you crack and overindulge.

If you answer no to _all_ of these, then you could consider adding a meal / tracker planner and calorie counter to your program.

Recap
1. While this chapter is essentially just for information, it would be beneficial to learn the role of each macro-nutrient.
2. Consider taking a DNA test like Fitness Genes through Spokes (a Spokes coach will analyse the results for you) or testing out different nutritional programmes to see if your body responds better to carbohydrates or fats, if it has a preference at all.
3. Consider mapping out how much protein your body needs per day. Carbohydrate and fat consumption will vary based on the nutritional programme you choose to follow, see chapter 12 *(page 106)* for more.

Chapter Eleven
Micro-nutrients

As mentioned in previous chapters, micro-nutrients are akin to the oil you'd put into your car[xxxvi]. They ensure your body runs smoothly. Micro-nutrients, sometimes called phyto-nutrients, are found in plants and some grains. Remember being told that an apple a day will keep the doctor at bay? Well there's a lot of truth in that! Lack of micro-nutrients is linked to a myriad of issues, such as bad skin, gut problems, brain fog, lack of energy, poor recovery and injury.

Bio-availability
People commonly use synthetic multi-vitamins to get micro-nutrients into their diets, although there is very little conclusive research to suggest this actually has any effect and many people now understand that such forms of vitamins aren't bio-available and therefore just expelled in the urine.

Being bio-available means your body is able to absorb the nutrients into the blood stream. It is possible to prove the bio-availability of multi-vitamin style products.

Supplementation
There are some non-synthetic products on the market that have research to show they are bio-available, although all research into any product should be taken with a pinch of salt as they may have been funded by the selling company, regardless of what peer reviewed or gold standard they may have attained.

I recommend using both common-sense and actual results or testimonials if you decide to supplement in this area. People who might supplement are those who cannot get sufficient intake in per day, this might be something as simple as not being able to eat enough, not having enough fruit and vegetables available (or suspect quality issues) or you are on a low carbohydrate diet, such as keto, which will restrict the amount you can eat.

Natural Sources

Micro-nutrition sources include fresh fruits, vegetables and some grains. It used to be considered that five servings of fresh fruit and vegetables a day would suffice, but the standard now is closer to 7-12 portions. However, if you are training, you probably need closer to 20. A portion is the size of your fist and the reason we need more comes down to the lack of nutrient density in our produce[xxxvii]. Modern farming techniques, regulations on crops and poor quality of soil all mean that we have lost the majority of the goodness from our produce.

I always use the banana as a perfect example. A yellow banana has the most nutrients in it, but most bananas are green when they reach the supermarket. Using this analogy, it's easy to see where we have gone wrong in growing our food. We simply lose so much of the nutrients from our produce when it is picked too early in order to reach the markets in sellable condition. In this respect, local produce trumps organic in terms of which is the more nutrient dense, but only, of course, if the local produce isn't packed full of chemicals. If you're not even close to consuming 20 portions per day, it's worth considering easy ways to get more micro-nutrients into your diet such as smoothies, juicing and snacking exclusively on fruit and vegetables.

If you've had a look at how many micro-nutrients there are, you'll know there are many and they are not all contained within each plant. You will need to eat a variety of plants I order to supply enough of each nutrient. The easiest way to do this is to think about eating the rainbow, no doubt you've heard about this. Typically, each colour of plant contains the same nutrients and therefore, when you eat all the colours of plants, you will satisfy your daily micro-nutrient intake needs.

Fresh or frozen fruit and vegetables will provide fibre as well as even more vitamins, minerals and antioxidants. Aim to choose from each colour group.

Red e.g. tomatoes, raspberries, strawberries
Purple e.g. black grapes, blueberries, figs
Orange e.g. carrots, oranges, mangoes
Green e.g. spinach, broccoli, fresh parsley
White e.g. cauliflower, mushrooms, onion

<u>One portion equals (size of your fist or 80g)</u>
- 3 heaped tbsp. of cooked vegetables
- 1 cereal bowl size full of salad
- 1 handful of leafy greens i.e. spinach
- 1 medium or 7 cherry tomatoes
- 1 medium fruit i.e. apple or orange
- 1 handful of berries or grapes
- 1 small banana or ½ mango
- 2 small fruits such as plums or kiwis
- 1-inch slice i.e. melon or pineapple

NB: not all fruit is created equally in terms of energy supply. The lowest in sugar and therefore the best for managing weight are; berries, cherries, apples, pears, plums, citrus.

The highest in sugar are mostly tropical fruits and are ideal post workout when sugar is needed for optimal recovery – bananas, mango, pineapples, melons and grapes.

Recap

1. Consider upping your intake of fruit and vegetables. Research what you have available and whether you can eat enough to avoid supplementation.

2. Using the information, you learnt in the previous chapter on what macro-nutrient your body prefers to fuel with (carbohydrate or fat) plan whether eating enough plants is possible.

3. If you have to supplement, ask your friends or seek testimonials on which one is best. Do some background research or ask a reputable coach for a recommendation.

Chapter Twelve
Specific nutritional programmes

The difference between 'your diet' and a 'diet' might not be anything but the way we perceive the word. 'Your diet' is simply what you eat, regardless of whether you are on a diet or nutritional programme. A 'diet' causes many people to stress out and that's why I prefer to call them 'Nutritional Programme'.

Whilst some athletes continually follow specific nutritional programmes for optimum health, such programmes are often just used to kick-start recovery from sub-par health. Listed over the following pages are the main ones that I would advise work well for endurance athletes, this list is non-exhaustive and ever changing, so there might be certain diets that didn't make this list and perfectly good for endurance athletes.

Check them out and, using the information you learned about yourself in the previous two chapters, make a decision about which one would best compliment your training needs. You might not need to jump straight in and sometimes a slow introduction to a diet is a good idea. Little steps are fine, providing you are heading towards an overall goal.

Give all diet programmes at least two weeks to work, but better a month if you can. Make adequate notes on how you feel, what your energy is like and how it has affected your performance.

Nutritionally Fit
I designed the Nutritionally Fit programme to support my athletes and those in endurance sports who are keen to ensure that what they put in to their bodies actually promotes adaptation and growth, helping them to become better, fitter and faster athletes. The Nutritionally Fit programme uses a lot of common sense, whole food nutrition and support. Much like my coaching, the

ethos has been slightly paraphrased to Truly Personalised Nutrition.

What I find most people sign up for, when they have chosen a programme like this, is the support and accountability. Almost everybody understands the difference between specific foods having a positive or negative effect on our bodies, what each of us needs is to be held accountable to actually following a truly nutritious diet. We have lots of resources for people to use within our programme, here is an extract from our on boarding guidelines.

"Diets do not work, lifestyle changes do. Short-term solutions are just that, short-term. The diet industry is forever trying to seduce us with their short-term solutions, telling us to drop weight fast with no thought on the impact that this sort of process has on our physical and mental wellbeing.

Do not think of my approach as another diet. This word is associated with negativity, deprivation and denial. Think of this as a subtle change to your current lifestyle. Whether you chose to jump in straight away following all the guidelines or you make one simple change every week or fortnight, you will see gains, you will feel great and your recovery will improve allowing you to train with more effectiveness at your next session.

I can't dictate to you what to eat, this decision starts in your head. What I can tell you is that the closer you follow these guidelines the easier it becomes to make smarter eating decisions. When you stabilize your blood sugar levels, your cravings will stop. Do not blame your circumstances, take full responsibility for your actions. Think about whether the next thing you eat will increase your time to recover or reduce it, base your decision on this.

If you don't like something or you're not enjoying what you are eating, then stop. Listen to your body. There is flexibility in these guidelines for you to follow. The same goes for your circumstances, there is flexibility for you to include your non-athletic family members, it is easy to fit in around even the most hectic lifestyles.

How you think is always more important than what you eat, because the right thoughts will guide you towards nourishing food. Saying you won't eat much today because you want to burn fat will find you starving hungry. But if you say you're going to eat sensibly today, starting with a good breakfast, your body will respond with energy to carry you through.

Your body is the greatest machine on earth and when you eat proper food it functions like a well-oiled engine. It responds to healthy eating because it's designed to do so. Ask yourself how you felt after you last ate junk food, you're in the minority if you say good!

The food suggested on this plan is natural. Proper, real food is freshly picked, gathered, hunted or fished and the further food strays from this basis, the unhealthier and the more confusing it becomes for your body.

We don't claim to be perfect; no human is. If you fall it is important to not feel negatively about this, dust yourself off and get back on the plan. If you need a day off don't consider this cheating, just consider it a little break. Listen to what your body is telling you, how does it feel after you eat junk food."

Nutritionally Fit became a free online resource in 2017. Based on Facebook (search for Spokes Nutritionally Fit), what you get is access to thousands of recipes, support from some amazing coaches, nutritionists and other athletes who have been through this experience and seen results so good they decided to also share their story.

We stand for making a diet work for you. Not all of the members of our support group follow my guidelines, but those that do see incredible results. The guidelines of NF are:

Saying YES to:
- Water – enough to keep your urine clear
- No Gluten
- No Dairy
- Relaxation – three times three minutes (deep breathing & calm) per day
- Sleep – 8 hours
- 5-6 Smaller Meals – fit them around your training
- Eating more plants; at least 12 portions of fruit and vegetables per day

Eliminating:
- Artificial Preservatives
- Artificial Colours
- Artificial Sweeteners
- Chemicals
- Caffeine
- Alcohol
- Refined Sugar
- Hydrogenated Fats

We put a lot of emphasis on how you eat and the mentality behind nutrition. Not fixating on a specific goal such as weight loss, but looking to become a healthier person. Never giving yourself a hard time when you 'cheat' and not considering it cheating at all! Simply acknowledging that you can be better and getting back on plan. Never making yourself feel bad for your choice. In this manner you are likely to last longer on this diet and have a great time supporting your training with correct nutrition.

Whole foods
This isn't necessarily a nutritional programme, but simply requires that you eat whole foods. 'Whole Foods' is defined as "food that has been processed or refined as little as possible and is free from additives or other artificial substances.". Some guidelines to consider are:

Saying YES to:
- Clean meats, seafood's and eggs
- Lots of vegetables and fruits
- Natural fats
- Foods with very few or no ingredients
- Foods with ingredients which you know
- No gluten nor dairy

Eliminating:
- Artificial Preservatives
- Artificial Colours
- Artificial Sweeteners
- Chemicals
- Caffeine
- Alcohol
- Refined Sugar

- Hydrogenated Fats

I would recommend that eating whole foods is worth testing as it is simple and common sense. Our bodies don't need processed foods; we survived for millions of years without them and can do so in our contemporary lives. Most of the guidelines are similar to those found in Nutritionally Fit.

The Whole30 programme is similar to a diet aimed at eating whole foods and provides more structure and comes as a ready-made package.

Palaeolithic diet (paleo)
The Paleo diet simply follows what we did in the days of the caveman. The main principle of this diet is that if it wasn't available back then, you shouldn't eat it. There are different levels of the paleo diet, which means that some of the food groups in the following categories might be open to interpretation as to where they should lie.

Foods to eat:
- Lean cuts of beef, pork, and poultry, preferably grass-fed, organic, or free-range selections
- Game animals, such as quail, venison, and bison
- Eggs, but no more than six a week, and preferably free-range
- Fish, including shellfish
- Fruit, such as strawberries, cantaloupe, mango, and figs
- Non-starchy vegetables, such as asparagus, onions, peppers, and pumpkin
- Nuts and seeds, including almonds, cashews, walnuts, and pumpkin seeds
- Olive oil, flaxseed oil, and walnut oil, in moderation

Foods to avoid:

- All dairy products, including milk, cheese, yogurt, and butter
- Cereal grains, such as wheat, rye, rice, and barley
- Legumes, like beans, peanuts, and peas
- Starchy vegetables, such as potatoes (and some even say sweet potatoes)
- Sweets, including all forms of candy as well as honey and sugar
- Artificial sweeteners
- Sugary soft drinks and fruit juices
- Processed and cured meats, such as bacon, deli meats, and hot dogs
- Highly processed foods

There are certain aspects of the paleo I really like; the idea of not eating anything processed will be a really benefit to your body. However, it is very restrictive and takes a lot of thoughts and preparation. I would recommend this if you have enough time to do meal prep.

Ketogenic diet (keto)
The keto diet has become one of the fastest growing nutritional programmes available. It makes a lot of sense for endurance athletes too; adapting your body to run more efficiently on its fat stores means you have an almost unlimited amount of fuel. Keto is a very low-carb, high-fat diet, that is very similar to the Atkins diet[xxxviii]. In essence, it shifts the body's metabolism from carbohydrates to fat and ketones. Ketones are produced in the liver from fat, when your body is in a state of 'ketosis', the result and requirement of the ketogenic diet.

To get the best benefits from a ketogenic diet, you must commit 100%, there's no opportunity to have the occasional 'cheat' day, nor does a slow introduction really work. It tends to be an all or nothing system. You can test whether you have achieved ketosis in a number of ways, typically this is via your urine.

Foods to Eat:
- Meat: Red meat, steak, ham, sausage, bacon, chicken and turkey.
- Fatty fish: Such as salmon, trout, tuna and mackerel.
- Eggs: Look for pastured or omega-3 whole eggs.
- Butter and cream: Look for grass-fed when possible.
- Cheese: Unprocessed cheese (cheddar, goat, cream, blue or mozzarella).
- Nuts and seeds: Almonds, walnuts, flax seeds, pumpkin seeds, chia seeds, etc.
- Healthy oils: Primarily extra virgin olive oil, coconut oil and avocado oil.
- Avocados: Whole avocados or freshly made guacamole.
- Low-carb veggies: Most green veggies, tomatoes, onions, peppers, etc.
- Condiments: You can use salt, pepper and various healthy herbs and spices.

Foods to Avoid:
Any food that is high in carbs should be limited.
- Sugary foods: Soda, fruit juice, smoothies, cake, ice cream, candy, etc.
- Grains or starches: Wheat-based products, rice, pasta, cereal, etc.
- Fruit: All fruit, except small portions of berries like strawberries.
- Beans or legumes: Peas, kidney beans, lentils, chickpeas, etc.
- Root vegetables and tubers: Potatoes, sweet potatoes, carrots, parsnips, etc.
- Low-fat or diet products: These are highly processed and often high in carbs.

- Some condiments or sauces: These often contain sugar and unhealthy fat.
- Unhealthy fats: Limit your intake of processed vegetable oils, mayonnaise, etc.
- Alcohol: Due to their carb content, many alcoholic beverages can throw you out of ketosis.
- Sugar-free diet foods: These are often high in sugar alcohols, which can affect ketone levels in some cases. These foods also tend to be highly processed.

There are two issues with the keto diet, the first is that due to its popularity, many companies/individuals have looked to take advantage by selling products or systems which simply do not work or follow the actual principle of fat adaptation. The second is that, with a very low-carb diet, you are restricted in the amount of plants you can eat. You might find that providing your body with enough micro-nutrients, especially when factoring in the research into diminished nutrient density of our produce (as mentioned above), is problematic and you should consider supplementing, if you choose to follow this diet.

My recommendation is to research thoroughly the right company or individual's advice to follow. Someone with extensive experience in implementing a keto diet amongst endurance athletes is necessary.

Gluten free
You may have noticed a common theme among the programmes listed above; everyone advocates a diet with no gluten nor dairy in it. Gluten is present in wheat, barley and rye (corn and oats have their own type of gluten so you wouldn't necessarily put these items in the gluten free bracket). The research into whether it is actually necessary to eliminate gluten from your diet is inconclusive. There is growing evidence to suggest that consuming gluten creates an inflammatory response in your gut with further reactions in your body[xxxix].

As an athlete, you want to rid your body of anything that creates inflammation. Give your body the best chance of recovering from exercise by not giving it something else to work on.

There's a lot to suggest that the chemicals that protect the crops are the issue but, without knowing for sure, the best advice is to test it out. Cut gluten out completely for 30 days and see how you feel. Almost everybody who has cut-out gluten successfully from their diets has experienced; better skin, better digestion, less brain fog, better sleep, less water retention, and many other factors.

Dairy free

In my personal opinion, it is best not to consume any dairy productions whatsoever. Much like gluten free, there is a lot of research and speculation as to whether or not it's healthier to observe a dairy free diet, but, as with a gluten free diet, I'd recommend trying it for 30 days to see how you feel.

Approximately 65% of the human population has a reduced ability to digest lactose after infancy[xl]. From gastro-intestinal distress to skin irritation, a whole myriad of symptoms are reduced when dairy is removed from almost everyone's diet, who have successfully given it up.

While I understand we once had a need for a cheap, easy to access food the majority of the world no longer has this issue. For me it is simple, you're not a baby cow!

Vegetarian and vegan

There is a lot of speculation as to whether athletes can support training on completely plant-based diet. It is more than possible; I know many cyclists who are more than capable of outperforming their peers whilst following a vegetarian or vegan diet.

This diet is simple, no meat products for vegetarians and in addition to that, no products produced by animals for vegan. There are different levels of each, for example pescetarianism allows you to eat fish but no other flesh. Strict vegans will go as far as to not eat honey, produced with the help of bees.

My recommendation is, if you wish to try this diet, to ensure that you get all the necessary amino-acids from plants. Be aware that you will need to eat a range of plants in order to achieve this. This is because essential amino acids (the ones our body can't make) are not as readily available in plant matter as they are in meat (meat having complete amino acid profiles). That being said, unless you are allergic to, or have problems digesting, soya or legumes you should be fine as these are readily available in most places worldwide.

Fuelling

If you really want to get the most from training and racing, then you'll need to get serious with your diet and commit to being the best you can be by seeing food primarily as fuel to promote good health and progress good performance. Of course, you need to enjoy what you eat but the key is to learn to enjoy what your body needs rather than what it craves. It's actually relatively easy to make enjoyable, nutritious food that will aid recovery and performance, but be aware that often it is only too easy to eat food that doesn't promote good health, but is so enjoyable that you eat it even though you know that it's just not helping you. I'm sure you will know which foods you personally would include in this category!

You might have identified yourself as someone who would respond better to a high fat diet, does this mean you need to go full keto? No. The programmes I mentioned above are merely guidelines into certain lifestyles, some incredibly restrictive and just not suitable to certain people. You can simply play around with your P / C / F ratio (Protein / Carbohydrate / Fat) until you find something that works really well for you.

Food addictions

Many people will suffer with some form of food addiction in their lifetime. The most addictive foods include sugar (it is more common to see carbohydrate addiction than ever!), unhealthy fats, processed food, salt and caffeine (I'm not including alcohol as a food!)[xli]. Your body craves these foods in the same way that a drug addict will crave a fix. The good news is that it is possible to change. Going cold turkey isn't the only way to approach giving something up, but, personally, I'd rather suffer for a few days then be done with it, rather than drag it out. Many like the 21-day approach. If you can go 21 days on a healthy nutritional programme, then you can go a lifetime. Once you begin to eat more healthily, you will crave healthier foods. It will be far less damaging to have the odd treat, and you'll feel better. It's a win-win situation. You'll find that if you can stabilise your blood sugar by dropping the amount of refined sugar you consume, eating healthily and exercising, you will crave less of the food that does you harm.

For performance

How a nutritional programme affects performance is very easy to test. Most people will already have a very good understanding of what they can and can't eat before a ride. I don't think I've met anyone who hasn't thought at least once about how food affects their performance. I also know enough people who can get away with eating one thing when their friends can't do it. Perfect café stop discussion really, but also take note of what other people eat. I know a lot of people will have coffee and cake, some will eat beans or egg on toast, there will be a real mix. Some will be eating for comfort and not performance, but most won't eat something they know will make their performance suffer on the return leg.

Eating for performance is different for everyone so it is paramount that you test what best suits you. Never leave it until the day or night before your big event to try something. There's plenty of opportunity to try things out, think about starting by just timing your food before training or a ride, keep a journal or diary and just write down what you have eaten, when you ate it and how you felt or performed during training or the ride.

You can immediately strike out anything that has a negative effect, unless you can say that poor performance could be due to another cause such as a cold, for example. With anything that works you should repeat the test to ensure that it wasn't a fluke or even due to other contributing factors.

Timing is everything, eating a giant meal less than an hour before a ride is almost certainly going to hurt. Similarly, not eating enough won't be pleasant either. A good starting guide is to eat your meal three hours before you get on the bike, you can then reduce or extend this depending on how it went. What you eat is personal choice, but low fat tends to be a good way to go, simply because it may sit in your stomach longer. High carbohydrate with protein is probably most people's preference, while porridge with fruit and a protein smoothie is also a good base to build on. In each case, you need to test which, if any, of these options suit you and to document the results.

If you are planning a ride with feed stops, consider what nutrition will be on offer. Find out and test it out, the last thing you want is to eat something that doesn't agree with you during the ride. You might also consider the cleanliness of the stops—all that food and drink, unrefrigerated and lying around, possibly in the sun, will that help or hinder your performance?

For recovery
Once you've trained you need to recover, one of my key factors in recovery is eating. Again, this is a perfect opportunity to try things out, but you might not notice the difference in recovery as quickly as you do the meal before your ride.

Now is the time to not eat too much! Too much will sit in your stomach and you won't feel great. It does need to be enough to kick start the recovery process and you should really be looking to include a balance of all the macros. Real food is best but if you aren't able to get that, maybe at an event, then a smoothie is perfect, lots of micro-nutrients from fruit, add some oats, seed or nut butter and then some protein mix.

If you are always fuelling correctly, then timing might not matter as much, but, within 45 minutes is the golden window to eat. Hit it and you stand to make your recovery and therefore adaptations quicker and stronger. If you want to see the biggest gains, ensure you give your body the best chance of recovering and being fit for your next session. If you have to eat junk at some point in the week then post ride is probably best when your body is looking for a quick hit. Having said that I always ask clients what's the point in doing all the work if they are going to undo it when they eat. Do you want muscles made of high-quality food or junky fast food?

For life

Unless you are a professional cyclist, you will probably have the occasional treat. I'm a realist and tell my clients that as long as it is a treat and not all the time; that they don't abuse it and they understand that it is not the best thing to do for performance, then it is ok. In some respects, it's actually refreshing to treat yourself occasionally, and can do the mind the world of good.

I subscribe to the 80:20 rule whereby if you eat healthfully 80% of the time then you can relax the other 20%. This way you get to enjoy a treat without it having too much of a bad effect. It all depends on how committed you are and what nutritional programme you are on. Most people would say that they are 100% committed, but a couple of months later they find that they have fallen off the wagon and it's more like 80% junk, 20% good. In these cases, it's almost certainly better to cheat in small doses to ensure you're committed the rest of the time. However, as you get closer to your event, when recovery and performance become even more crucial, the 80:20 rule should probably be adjusted to nearer 90:10.

As mentioned earlier, the closer you stick to being perfect the easier it becomes. As your blood sugar levels stabilise, cravings will reduce. At some point you will look at sugary, fatty treats and think no thank you! This might be hard to believe but try it, what do you have to lose?

Fasted training

Fasted training is great when applied correctly. However, too many people either go too hard or too long, or a combination of both, all in the pursuit of losing weight. If you wish to lose weight, it is far better to do so with a planned diet. While you may lose weight when following a fasted training programme, it is not the prime reason for undertaking it. For example, if you are time-strapped, then fasted training can be a good base to build upon—you just need to ensure that you consequently replenish some carbohydrates and get enough protein in.

I would suggest that, until you are used to it, you keep fasted training to an hour or less. With just an hour the body shouldn't begin to crave uncontrollably, whereas if you go any longer you might struggle with cravings all day. Once you are used to it, you can start to complete fasted training for longer than an hour. Try to keep training to a lower intensity—emptying your glycogen stores is a fairly horrible experience and, again, one that will almost certainly mean you will experience severe cravings after your session. That said, if you are looking primarily to boost your performance then glycogen depleted training can provide some terrific gains because you are forcing your body to run on no carbs so it's having to fuel via fat. Getting your body efficient at burning fat for fuel will give you an infinite resource for energy when you really need it.

Always ensure you are protecting your body with adequate protein. The lack of fuel might tempt your body to cannibalise your muscles, undoing all your hard work.

It's worth noting that it becomes incredibly hard to use any method of monitoring performance and recovery when doing fasted training. Holding a certain power output will be considerably harder when training on empty, you will be getting a different adaptation and, if you use systems like Training Stress Score (TSS) in TrainingPeaks, there's no current way to factor in the added recovery time unless you simply add it yourself.

Recap
1. Using the information, you learned on yourself in the previous chapter, identify whether there is a specific nutritional method or programme that might support your body most.
2. Consider if you have any allergies or intolerances when making a decision.
3. Once you have decided, do adequate research to the point you understand fully what that programme entails, the rules, restrictions and the benefits.

Chapter Thirteen
Hydration

There's been some recent scientific research that suggests that cramping isn't caused by lack of electrolytes at all and is, in fact, a result of severe fatigue[xlii]. If you've ever experienced cramping, try to think about the time that it occurred. Maybe you'll find that overtraining is the cause of your cramping. Either way, I do recommend that my clients drink an electrolyte solution while riding, particularly during long or intense sessions or in heat. I'll touch on the role of heat, for dehydration, more in chapter 24 *(page 198)*.

You can probably Google a number of general theories that might either help or lead you astray when working out how much you should drink per hour. What I want to do is to teach you how to figure it out for yourself.

The oldest method is to weigh yourself before and then immediately after training. The general rule is 24 fluid ounces (700 ml) of fluids for every pound (0.45 kg) of body weight you lose. There are calculators online, although these are not particularly personalised. You can get sweat testing done, Precision Hydration[xliii], for example, do this (check out their electrolyte formula too – the only sports nutrition product that I actually recommend). This involves simply attaching electrodes to your arm which promote sweating. The results can be measured in fluid volume and sodium content. This can be a valuable figure to show how much you need to drink and what concentrate of electrolytes you may want.

Dehydration and hyponatremia (drinking too much fluids) can have catastrophic effects on performance, not to mention the risk of severe illness[xliv]. Find out what works for you by monitoring your performance in training and then play around with the concentration of electrolytes or the quantity of fluids you drink. If you use a power meter, this will be fairly easy to understand. If you are using heart rate you will need to measure your hydration and electrolytes by other methods too. A common problem with being dehydrated is that you will experience a higher heart rate, while drinking too much might cause upset stomach (you might also need to visit the toilet more frequently!).

Check your urine after every ride. Really, it shouldn't look too far from slightly off-clear. If you get back and it's a dark colour, you need more fluids. On hot days, don't make the mistake of thinking you need more energy in your bottle, you need more water and electrolytes. Get your energy from food and allow your body to use what's in your bottle to cool you down.

The perfect home-made electrolyte drink is a simple one. Start with one-part organic apple juice (any juice will do, whatever you have available – but actually just juice, plus organic is better!) to three parts water. Then add a pinch of salt to your bottle. That's it, simple, cheap and effective. It's also very easy to modify for personal need. Getting cramp twinges? Add more salt. Urine darker than normal? Add more water and reduce juice. Make it work for you.

Commonly people do one of two things. They either drink too much or too little. With performance fluctuating widely between being adequately hydrated and not, it really doesn't serve you to get it wrong. Just test it out, get it sorted now and don't worry about it. Increase when it gets warmer and don't forget to drink when it's cooler, that is quite easy!

If you're riding time trials and you know you sweat heavily, having a bottle on a 25-mile time trial, while unconventional, will bring you more gains than being dehydrated[xlv]. Being dehydrated will sap energy and destroy your performance, being aero won't help if the engine isn't running.

Another big mistake people make is to try to train your body to use less fluids. In my experience, this just isn't possible, you're just setting yourself up for a feeling rubbish and risking sickness. You are much better off spending your time trying to adapt more to the heat, again see chapter 24 *(page 198)*.

Recap

1. Conduct a test to determine how much fluid and electrolyte you need per hour for a normal ride or session.
2. Make notes when it gets hotter as to how much more you need to drink.

Chapter Fourteen
Food sources

Not everything that is sold as fresh in supermarkets is actually fresh and, even when it is, it might not be that good for you. Creative and colourful advertising from supermarkets has given us a false impression that what is being sold is actually healthy, whereas the truth is that in many cases this is misleading. In the pursuit of getting you the fruit and vegetables you need, farmers supplying the supermarkets have to pick their produce far too early which causes a loss of nutrient density.

Unfortunately, there's more bad news. Mass-production farming methods such as the abandonment of arable farming (in which soil is allowed to regenerate, and nutrients re-filter) alongside rulings that state produce must look good, forces farmers to breed strains for factors such as appearance and yield over nutrition. All these factors mean that the density of the micro-nutrients in our produce has dropped drastically over the last 50-60 years.

The following studies all found an alarming decrease in nutrient density over a variety of different minerals from a variety of different produce.

One of the earlier studies to break news of this trend was published in 2004 by Donald Davis. Entitled *Changes in USDA food composition data for 43 garden crops, 1950 to 1999*, the paper shows the results of the density of 43 garden crops for 13 nutrients and how the data changed between 1950 and 1999. The results show that for six nutrients—protein, calcium, phosphorus, iron, riboflavin (Vitamin B2), and ascorbic acid (Vitamin C)—the decline was between 6% (for protein) and 38% (for riboflavin).

A *British Food Journal* study on nutrient density from 1930 to 1980 found that in 20 different vegetables the average potassium content had dropped 14%, calcium content 19%, and iron content

22%. In general, the comparison of mineral content over this period shows significant reductions in magnesium, iron, copper, and potassium in fruit—and calcium, magnesium, copper, and sodium in vegetables.

Another study by Kushi Institute uncovered the same alarming trend. When analysing nutrient levels in food based on USDA data from 1975 to 1997, it was found that Vitamin A levels had decreased 21%, calcium levels 27%, Vitamin C levels 30%, and iron levels 37%.

One more study, reported by the Toronto Globe and Mail in 2002, analysed food tables prepared by scientists between 1951 and 1999. It showed marked decreases in the nutrient levels in fruits and vegetables bought in Canadian supermarkets, and showed that potatoes had lost 100 percent of their Vitamin A and 57 percent of their Vitamin C, and even concluded that today's consumers would have to eat eight oranges to get the same amount of Vitamin A that their grandparents gained from eating one orange!

Buy local
How do you solve this? My advice is to seek out local farmers' markets—they are great for buying local produce. Local produce will have more nutrients than non-local, and supporting your local community is an added bonus. Shortening the supply chain will lead to the crops being fresher and picked at a more optimal time.

It's so much better for you and for the farmer. If you are unable to buy from a local farmers' markets, then it's worth noting that frozen produce might contain less pesticides than fresh because they don't need to be rushed to the store and will be picked at the peak of ripeness. In this way, you're buying 'local' even if it's shipped frozen. Of course, there's an inherent risk that a given produce hasn't been looked after in the delivery chain, but there's not a lot you can do about that and it might be a risk worth taking.

Grow your own
You might consider this unlikely, maybe you have no garden, no access to an allotment or simply not enough time. Well, you don't need to be a farmer to grow your own food, you don't even need a garden. Systems like hydroponics or aeroponics bring the farm into the home (or onto the patio – light dependant).

"Hydroponics is a subset of hydroculture, which is a method of growing plants without soil by using mineral nutrient solutions in a water solvent. Terrestrial plants may be grown with only their roots exposed to the mineral solution, or the roots may be supported by an inert medium, such as perlite or gravel" – Wikipedia.

"Aeroponics is the process of growing plants in an air or mist environment without the use of soil or an aggregate medium. The word "aeroponic" is derived from the Greek meanings of aer and ponos. Aeroponic culture differs from both conventional hydroponics, aquaponics, and in-vitro growing" – Wikipedia.

Systems might yield up to 30% more produce, 3x faster and, in the case of aeroponics, with 98% less water[xlvi]. It is simple and effective and because you control what goes into it, you can keep it healthy and harvest it at the peak of its freshness.

Organic
If you can buy local and also organic, that's even better, but be aware that the common misconception is that organic food is pesticide-free whereas in fact it is just much more controlled, with some pesticides reduced and certain ones or methods banned. So, despite the considerably higher cost, you are still consuming some toxins that will be harming your body. These chemicals are sometimes misplaced within organic food by spray drifting from nearby non-organic farms. It is also estimated that some samples, in the following example, are present due to mislabelling or even fraud.

That said, organic food does tend to contain less than a third of the toxins found in non-organically grown produce. A Consumers Union research into whether organic foods really do have less pesticides found that:

"73% of conventionally grown foods had at least one pesticide residue, while only 23% of organically grown samples of the same crops had any residues. More than 90% of the USDA's samples of conventionally-grown apples, peaches, pears, strawberries and celery had residues, and conventionally-grown crops were six times as likely as organic to contain multiple pesticide residues. The California data (based on tests with less sensitive detection limits) found residues in 31% of conventionally grown foods and only 6.5% of organic samples, and found multiple residues nine times as often in conventional samples. CU tests found residues in 79% of conventionally grown samples and 27% of organically grown samples, with multiple residues ten times as common in the former. The levels of residues found in organic samples were also consistently lower than levels of the same pesticides found in conventional samples, in all three sets of residue data."

However, there's no need to fear non-organic food neither, as the content very rarely gets close to the limits that national bodies consider unsafe. Non-organic food simply contributes to the amount of work your body has to do to remove toxins. The harder your body has to work on removing toxins from your body, the less it has available to recover from training.

Seasonal
Should we prioritise eating fresh produce when it is in season? The answer lies in considering the supply chain. If you eat produce when it is in season in your local area, you need to know how far it has actually travelled and whether it was at peak ripeness when it was picked. This will help to inform you on its nutritional value — buying seasonally and local should mean you are getting produce at the peak of their freshness.

However, if you eat only seasonal produce you might miss out on the breadth of beneficial micro-nutrients available in the variety of colours on offer. A great way to think about variety is to 'eat the rainbow', i.e. as many different coloured fruit and vegetables as possible. The range of colours in fresh produce and, in particular anything brightly-coloured, will have a wide and varied list of micro-nutrients that will be of benefit to you, so, where possible, eat a wide variety of in-season goods... it's as simple as that!

Recap
1. Using the guidelines of the nutritional programme, or diet, you chose, create a shopping/grocery list of items you'll need to buy.
2. Where possible, try to source these items in this order:
   a. Seasonal.
   b. Local.
   c. Organic.
3. Consider aeroponics as a solution to getting enough fresh fruit and vegetables.

Chapter Fifteen
Supplementation

I am a big fan of getting all my nutrients from whole foods and I always pass this recommendation on to my athletes. My belief is that there are only a few good reasons to use supplements—also, I doubt that many of those on the market are bio-available. By this I mean that, once you ingest it, the product actually enters the blood stream and isn't simply passed in your urine (as is the case with many multi-vitamins).

That said, if your doctor has prescribed a dietary supplement for you it's probably for good reason and you need to take it. I am not in a position to disagree with the advice of any doctor, but I have been in a personal situation where I was told that taking a certain medicine would improve my quality of life. I disagreed, sought natural methods and today I am far healthier with zero of the side effects I would have received going down the synthetic remedy route.

The only supplements I take are plant-based, and have been proven to support an active lifestyle. For example, I recommend a plant-based omega fatty acid capsule if you don't eat much fish and, even if you do, it's worth checking how much against guidelines about the required quantity. If you include enough oily fish in your diet, then you may not need an omega fatty acid supplement.

Similarly, there are other reasons you would supplement. If you are a vegan who has an intolerance to soya or legumes it might be recommended to eat a lysine as it is commonly lacking in a vegan diet. If you can't eat soy or legumes you will be very restricted by the amount of this essential amino acid that you can get through your diet.

If you live in a part of the world where sunlight becomes sparse during winter, then a vitamin D supplement might be a good idea as there a few foods that contain this and you naturally produce it with the help of sunlight. Vitamin D plays a critical role in forming and maintaining healthy bones. It also helps keep your muscles, nerves and immune system healthy.

One of the first questions I ask new clients is what supplements they are taking. This question is quickly followed by asking what they think that supplement is doing for them and exploring why they think they can't get the nutrients it contains from food. There might be a very good reason to use a certain supplement, but in most cases, fixing your diet is a far better, and healthier, way to achieve the same results.

I also get questioned a lot about the use of legal performance enhancing supplements such as high doses of caffeine, creatine, beta alanine and sodium bicarbonate to name a few. I can't envisage a day where I become a coach who tells any of my clients to use a product that contains anything synthetic, non-organic or untested. Even if you can source high doses of these supplements in a natural way, without altering it through process, I'd prefer to look for other ways to help my clients improve. There might be an argument for it if you're at your peak level or a professional, that's it though!

Sorry to those of you who were hoping to read something about legal performance enhancing drugs!

Part Two – Recap
If you have followed this part correctly, you will now have:

1. Found out what source of fuel your body prefers, if any.
2. Increased your intake of fruit (depending on nutritional programme) and vegetables.
3. Identified a specific approach to your nutrition, be that a programme or general outline.
4. Developed your hydration strategy.

5. Created a shopping/grocery list of foods that suit your new nutritional programme.
6. Finally using this chapter:
   a. Using both your guidelines for your nutritional programme and what your local stores have available, construct a list of likely needs for supplementation.
   b. Research and find the best supplements.

Congratulations! You are now two quarters of the way through this book and, if you implement your plan correctly, 50% closer (15% training and 35% nutrition) to achieving your cycling goals!

Part Three
Mentality

'In order to succeed, we must first believe we can' (Nikos Kazantzakis)

Introduction

For me, one's mental attitude to cycling is where things fall apart for many aspiring athletes (and, to the same extent, even for professional cyclists). In my experience, mental attitude is accountable for around 50% of all your gains, with nutrition making up 35% and the training itself only around 15%. My personal view is that if you are not taking your sport seriously—if you are not committed enough, if you can't stay the course or you can't push past the pain—then you will never reach your full potential. However, the first thing to consider is what level of commitment you are actually aiming to achieve. Some people will sacrifice a huge amount to achieve their goals, but, for most, athletic goals need to work around overall lifestyle. So, if goal setting is not your first priority, how do you train in earnest? What is the secret?

Case study

Claire Goldsmith is a casual cyclist who accidentally signed up to complete the multi-day TransAlp event—a gruelling seven-day challenge covering over 500 km with 18000 m altitude difference from start to end. She had no aspirations of winning, solely the simple goal of completing the event by the cut-off time. Early on, it became apparent that the performance aspect of Claire's training would not be the main issue; it was her belief in herself that was truly holding her back. Claire and I spent a lot of time on the phone talking through every aspect of her training, looking at the reasons why she was entering the race, and changing anything that wasn't working for her in order to ensure that she didn't just achieve her goal because she was capable of physically completing the event, but also to help her believe in herself—to believe that she could mentally rise to the challenge. In July 2015, she completed the event without even getting close to being near to the cut-off time.

It might help if I give you some background on my own mental health journey.

Ever since I was a child, I had issues with my behaviour and mood. As I entered into my teens this started presenting itself as intense anxiety, with regular panic attacks and outbursts of violent behaviour. I had no idea that what I was feeling wasn't normal.

To escape this negative pattern, I started experimenting with drugs and alcohol. This soon became an addiction, which despite several attempts I wasn't able to shift in my early twenty's. More abnormal behaviour and outbursts led me to start looking into what was happening in my mind. I was incorrectly diagnosed by my GP as Clinically Depressed and was visited as an outpatient by the local mental health team after having some low mood, suicide attempts and self-harm.

Unfortunately, the support from NHS was not enough and after a couple of particularly nasty incidents I was diagnosed with Bipolar Affective Disorder. At one time I spent a couple of weeks in psychiatric care to help break that pattern of behaviour.

Recovery
What is the best way to overcome any form of addiction? Replace it with something else. When I gave up my life of drinking, drugs, poor diet and negative attitude I replaced it with exercising. Later this became cycling training and my love affair with nutrition started because I needed to lose weight. I didn't realise it at the time, but nutrition would become one of the cornerstones of maintaining my mental stability.

As the weight came off and my cycling legs came back (they had been missing nearly a decade!) I soon found myself becoming a strong cyclist again. At first my determination and motivation came from wanting to prove to myself that I could do it, that I wasn't a failure and that it was possible for someone like me to be a productive member of society. Later, when I was introduced to time trialling, that became wanting to beat myself.

I worked hard and I studied a lot. I learnt how to convert a decade of coaching and people management experience, from a food retail environment, into one relevant to the cycling industry. My business was founded upon my belief that everyone should get a unique, yet outstanding client experience. This saw my business grow faster than I could ever expect and today it operates in over 20 different countries, with an amazing team of people around me who help guide it.

One of my proudest days was being able to go professionally into cycling coaching and support myself. I had figured out exactly how to maintain my mental health through exercise (training), nutrition and having my business as a purpose to work hard remaining stable. Life was good again, I even managed to taper off the medication which had helped me find stability when I was first diagnosed.

Yet, something was missing. In analysing my life, I could time every severe manic episode with the breakdown of a romantic relationship and such in the five years I worked on myself and transformed from an overweight addict into a functioning member of society, I had hidden away from any romantic attachment. I had allowed myself to become a recluse, unable to communicate my issues and hiding that I had a mental disability, mainly due to the stigma attached to it.

I had the opportunity to spend a winter in California with some good friends. Sadly, my trip wasn't plain sailing and I spent one of the longest periods of my life swinging between mania and depression. I had to learn to talk to people about my problems. This felt incredibly hard to begin with. Thoughts like "what will they think?", "can I trust them?" and "what if they use it against me?" filled my mind. But the saying is true, practice makes perfect. Not long after I had told those first handful of people, I was recording a video that I shared on Facebook, which was viewed by tens of thousands of people.

One of the first people who I talked to was a woman who I had met through a nutrition business we were both involved in. We actually met on a video call with 10 other people in February 2016, I remember looking at her and smiling, a smile lit up her face. In turn this made me smile more, and so did she. We met in person in Phoenix at a conference March 2016. We spoke frequently between that time and when I visited her in Northern California December 2016. We had our first date January 1st 2017 but had very limited time together due to VISA restrictions. We fell in love via Facetime.

Noelle has become my rock, my muse, my inspiration. She taught me to love myself, to meditate and made me feel supported. With all aspects of my life complete; training, nutrition, relaxation and support I have finally found inner peace. No doubt this will be tested in the future, but for now I enjoy the tranquillity of un-medicated good mental health.

Chapter Sixteen
Healthy living

Quick note: At this point, you will need your list of commitments from chapter 2 *(page 20)*. If you need a reminder, head back to chapter 2. You might find it interesting to go through your list of commitments again.

It's important to understand that the mental side of training is tied heavily to nutrition. I'd take it one step further still and suggest that every single aspect of your daily lifestyle—the choices you make—will have an effect on your health. Smoking, drinking alcohol, taking drugs, being exposed to various pollutants, the quality of the water you drink, levels of hygiene, your social life, work life, stress levels, and quality of sleep—all of these factors, plus dozens more, determine your overall health. You don't have to be 100% all of the time, but the closer you can get to holistic health perfection the better you will feel and the better you will perform.

Healthy living is much more than training, racing or weight loss—it is a way of life. I firmly believe that people should never lose weight to be healthy, but that in being healthy they'll lose weight. The same goes for racing and training, take your health back and just see how much better you perform. Make every moment count. Ask yourself whether the decision you are about to make will reduce or increase the quality of your overall health. Will taking the stairs help you reach your next key session or will taking the elevator be a better option? If you are training, and in particular if you are close to an A event, you should seriously be focusing on making every moment help your body. This includes throwing away the rule book and being lazy if that will be of benefit to you!

Yes, some of this might be in complete contradiction to everything we are normally taught. But, you're in training for something special. You are not the average couch potato, who does very little to no physical activity. You need as much of your life to line up and compliment your training as is possible. If you're pro or have targets that are very high, you might need *everything* to line up.

Quality of sleep

Probably one of the biggest factors in recovery and adaptation is the quality of your sleep. The quality of sleep isn't just about the amount of time that we sleep—it's also about the nature of our sleep. The optimum time to aim for is 8 hours if you are training, but you also need to consider factors such as comfort, warmth, light and quietness, as well as stress levels, that affect the quality of your sleep[xlvii].

How do you make the most from your sleep? Well I might not be telling you any new information here. First of all, put any artificial lights away long before you plan on getting into bed. If you have to, and I mean have to, then look to getting filters that will reduce or remove certain lights from your vision. Try to put your phone down at least an hour before you go to sleep, this does the same for anything like television or your computer. Even if you typically fall asleep fast, you might still be disrupting your sleep by focusing on something later into the night.

The same goes for stress. You do really need to relax more before getting into bed. This could mean that you have some quiet, alone time before bed. Maybe that looks like a hot bath with Epsom salts. Maybe you meditate. Try to never go to bed in a bad mood, you'll sleep poorly and wake up feeling the same. Chill.

Your environment will make a huge difference in the quality of your sleep too. Is it too noisy, can you reduce this at all? Will light disturb you, can you put up some light reducing blinds? Will you be too warm or too cold? Spend some time figuring out exactly how you like to sleep. Use tracking software on your phone to record the length and quality of your sleep, correlate this to the influences just mentioned to work out exactly what environment you need to sleep.

Cleanliness of your bed... yep, you need to sleep on clean sheets, with a supportive mattress. Dirt might disturb your breathing during the night, not to mention if you get some sort of bed bug infestation.

You can even extend this to cleanliness of your bedroom. A cluttered, disorganised room might provide the perfect environment for a bad night sleep. I'll not go into much detail in this book, but you could consider reading up on Feng Shui[xlviii]. Again, it's very little effort and could produce a positive result. Let's be honest, even if it's not backed by science, it won't hurt!

Even consider having a separate napping routine. Getting a nap in after training might be the best way to promote recovery. Many professional sportspeople are now turning to a well thought out napping routine to gain the edge on their opponents. Factor in the same influences when creating your planned nap routine and test out how long you need. In most cases it is less than thirty-minutes.

A worthwhile note about napping, your boss might not approve of you doing it at work, although an argument could be made for increased productivity. Depending on how approachable your employer is, you could tentatively float this idea, emphasising that you will be able to work harder post-nap and that you can compensate for time lost by staying late. Better yet, if you can get away with it and then prove the results you could skip the conversation altogether. Sometimes an apology that brings good news is better than asking a question on deaf ears.

Whether you like this idea or not, there's no harm is it in trying for a week or two, just to see how you feel? Much like your nutrition, sometimes you'll have a bigger benefit from doing this than another person. This could be a massive game changer for you.

Stress levels

Another major factor in the level of your performance is stress. Ask yourself when was the last time you had a really stressful day, when did you last feel as if you were being crushed, as if the weight of the world was bearing down on you. How often do you feel overwhelmed by how much you have on your plate with very little time in which to do it; that you have too much going on with no end in sight? During this time, how well did you train, or did you even train at all? Many people will admit that they didn't train at all, or that they trained poorly. However, some will acknowledge how they felt and turn it into renewed motivation; changing a negative situation into a positive outcome. Those are the people who improve next time they test.

Not everyone has the capacity or willingness to turn stress into a positive motivator and, even if you can, it's far better to attempt to reduce your stress levels as much as possible rather than continually pushing through it. You'll be happier and you'll live longer. You'll never get rid of stress completely and, in some respects, it's entirely necessary to function as a human being, but overall, reducing your stress levels will result in improved health.

Think about how you feel when you are training, then think about how you feel when you are very stressed. There are a lot of similarities in the way the body is behaving; elevated heart rate, loss of focus or presence, sweating, other mental aspects. Then think about what we want to achieve when you are not training – recovering. It's simple, the more relaxed you are outside of training, the more focus your mind and body can give to recovering from said training.

Once you've successfully reduced stress to a manageable level, you can set to work on learning how to manage it. Like I mentioned above, you definitely do not want to rid yourself of stress. Stress will ensure you work hard in order to pay your bills. Stress will help you train harder to achieve your goals. Stress might help you lose weight. But stress will only do this, once you learn to manage it.

Meditation is probably the best method to learning to manage stress. If you've never meditated before, try the Headspace app. It's simply 10 minutes per day, and might change your life. I really doubt you can say you don't have 10 minutes per day, after all you're reading this book, aren't you? How many minutes per day on average do you read, or look on social media, or watch television?

Sickness and injury
At the time of writing, I've not had a cold, bug or illness worth mentioning in around four years. I put this down to very clean living, flooding my body with as many micro-nutrients as possible every day and taking other contributing precautions. For example, sometimes I get to the point where I've been out for a long ride and my body is feeling tired, perhaps I'm feeling as though I'm getting a sniffle or a cough, a couple of sneezes but that is it, I never get any worse.

The more training stress you put your body under, the more likely you are to get sick. You can take precautions; ensuring you eat a balanced diet full of quality ingredients and getting all the necessary macro and micro-nutrients into your body. But also think about external influences; washing your hands regularly or washing your food before you eat it (even if it says pre-washed). What about other people? Try to identify when your body feels like it will get sick, this can be at the end of a big block of training, after a very tough session or ride, maybe it's even in your recovery week. Once you know this, can you start to avoid certain influences? Mainly these are other people, especially children. It's not that hard to do, just consider that if you do get ill, you might have to spend more time at home anyway. If you can't avoid people, can you simply avoid contact with them? I always tell my athletes, after they've raced, to treat everyone like they have some horrible contagious disease, no handshakes, no hugs and if anyone asks, maybe you're the one with the slight cold...

Injuries occur when the body cannot adapt to the stimulus you are putting it under. So, if you cause your body to be under too much stress, with too much volume or intensity, you will become sick or you will suffer an injury. This is where a qualified coach is a valuable asset. Being able to read the warning signs, removing bias and understanding the principle roles of all the body's systems equate to far less risk of sickness or injury.

What are the warning signs? Some are really obvious like a niggle in one of your muscles, maybe a joint is hurting and there's no reason for that, maybe you just aren't feeling that great. If you are using a system like TrainingPeaks, you probably have a complete record of all your previous training and injuries. Armed with that you can work out exactly how much training is too much. Maybe you got injured after a very hard week of training. Maybe it is cumulative over a few months. Maybe you skipped the crucial preparation phase after a week or two off the bike. If you don't have this data, then start saving it! Regular notes on your training and how you feel are gold. Using an app like HRV4Training can also help too, just one minute every morning, a few further questions and you have all the info you need to correlate your injury risk.

What can we do to decrease your injury risk? Start with an adequate stretching routine. Maybe you include some yoga, Pilates or other similar sessions into your training. Maybe your gym strength work also compliments what you have been doing and if you have that previous data, you have an indication of what weaknesses your body might have and areas to strengthen.

The next step up from that would be regular visits to a qualified sports therapist or physiotherapist. These professionals will identify any areas where injuries may occur. A sports therapist will easily be able to tell if your training is imbalanced and they might give you some exercises to take away to work on. Regular sports massages or the use of a foam roller might reduce muscle damage, help flush the lymphatic system and increase the body's ability to recover.

It's worth me finalising this section by saying that nothing is going to guarantee that you don't get sick or injured, all you can do is take precautions. If you do get sick, you must allow your body time to recover. Seek professional help and be honest with yourself. Too many people train while sick or injured and it causes the issue to get worse. At best you might simply drag out the problem even longer. Try to take 2-3 days getting back into your training for each day you lose. If you lose more than a week, consider starting back at the beginning again and doing another preparation phase.

Relaxation

Relaxation is an excellent method of aiding recovery, so it is important to consider what helps you to relax. You might find, for example, that taking time out from work or family commitments — or even training commitments — can contribute enormously to helping you relax and thus ensure that you are mentally fit throughout the season and, indeed, in the whole of life.

Burn-out (mental fatigue) occurs when your mind is no longer able to recover from the stimulus you are placing it under in your daily life. Workload, family and social commitments, training, racing — everything contributes to your mental fatigue and, at some point, you will find that you are not be able to continue, much in the way that chronic fatigue affects the body.

One thing that might help you to relax is meditation. As mentioned previously, you could try Headspace[xlix] or you could try something like yoga. Both will help you relax, take your mind away from the stresses of the outside world and help you to feel free from the stresses of everyday life. This time away from daily concerns has helped me to overcome many potential bouts of burn-out.

Meditation doesn't suit everyone, but I advise you to try yoga, Pilates, or something similar to see if it has a positive effect on your life and on your athletic performance. You might also try simply sitting in a quite space alone and just allowing your thoughts to pass through your head. Meditation can be used for anything—more quality sleep, removing or dealing with stress, athletic performance, recovery, you name it you can train your brain to deal with it better.

If meditation just sounds too much or even too 'out there' for you right now, why not simply try some breathing exercises:

1. Sit or lie flat in a comfortable position.
2. Put one hand on your belly just below your ribs and the other hand on your chest.
3. Take a deep breath in through your nose, and let your belly push your hand out.
4. Breathe out through pursed lips as if you were whistling.
5. Do this breathing 3 to 10 times.

Start here and see how you feel. There are many apps that can help you with guided exercises and you can do them anytime, anywhere.

Once you've settled on your regime, the next step is to turn that into routine. Create the habit and commit to doing it every day. Don't beat yourself up if you miss a day, use this as motivation to ensure that you get back on track the following day. First thing in the morning might be the best time to do this, start your day right.

If you are able to do so, one of the most effective ways to relax is to simply remove yourself from significant triggers. For example, if you have a certain friend who has a knack of bringing you down, sucking your energy or turning your mental wellbeing from positive to negative, then the simple solution would be to remove them from your life. This may sound harsh but I'm a firm believer in Jim Rohn's philosophy that you become the average of the five people you most hang around with. If you surround yourself with negative people, you will become a negative person. If you surround yourself with successful people, you will become successful. You can apply this to many aspects of your life. If your work has a negative effect on your life, change your job. If you are in a dead end, unhappy relationship, consider why it is that you persevere with that relationship. It's worth bearing in mind that Einstein's definition of insanity is to repeat the same process over and over again and expect a different outcome. You are the master of your destiny; make a change that will positively affect your life and, ultimately, your performance.

Chemicals

Chemicals are *everywhere*, not just in the food you eat. Consider the advice I gave in the nutrition part; your body is trying to recover and adapt from the training stress you are putting it under. Giving it more to do, in this case removing toxins from the body, might just slow your ability to recover and improve. The following mentioned factors might not affect everyone, and I could write a whole, probably rather boring, book on everything that contains chemicals that you really don't want in your body. But here are the main ones, hopefully it'll also get you thinking about all the chemicals you might be exposing your body too.

Toothpaste, yes seriously, this actually might be the one that is doing you the most damage. It will depend on what the manufacturers are allowed to add to their paste in your part of the world, but there are a lot of very damaging ingredients in common versions. Again, this might depend on whether a warning is mandatory where you live rather than if it is a consideration, go check your toothpaste right now, does it have a warning on there that states to not ingest? Unless you're using a natural paste, it probably does or probably should. Now consider that, although you might not sallow your toothpaste, it still goes into your mouth. Some might get digested; some might get absorbed into the mouth and the rest might change the acidity of your mouth and stomach. Did you know that your toothpaste frothing up is irrelevant to the cleaning process and actually only present for marketing?

Again, this might depend a lot on where you live, but, do not drink tap water! While most places in the world class their water as 'safe' this doesn't mean they are chemical free. Here are some chemicals that might typically be found in your water supply[1]:

- Chlorine.
- Fluorine compounds.
- Trihalomethanes (THMs).
- Salts of arsenic, radium, aluminium, copper, lead, mercury, cadmium and/or barium.
- Hormones.
- Nitrates.
- Pesticides.

The pipes transporting your water might not be that safe neither; there might be up to 8% lead in 'lead free' pipes. While you might not actually get sick from drinking your tap water, you might consider giving your body a hand by filtering it. Please do not buy bottled water, it is an incredible drain on the environment. Either filter it in your home or purchase it from a store in a large reusable container, some areas you can get it delivered.

Not that I'm trying to scare you, but, if you're going to filter your tap water, you might want to filter your bathing water too. You might actually absorb more chlorine by having a long shower or bath than you do through drinking tap water. If you have any skin issues, dry or itchy skin, eczema or anything similar, a shower filter is an easy and convenient that might relieve some of the symptoms.

Finally consider your cosmetics such as your shampoo, body wash and laundry detergent. Much like toothpaste, these have added ingredients which are cheap to manufacture. While you might smell great, you are still exposing your body to unnecessary toxins. Go organic, shop around and find something plant based. It does the job the same and you might feel better for it.

Food
I'm not going to spend much time here, just simply remind you to check chapter 14 *(page 125)* when making decisions about your food intake.

Air quality
Depending on where you are in the world, your government might have an 'air quality' website. You can log into this and check previous data, current quality and many other factors. Of course, unless you're planning on moving, there's really very little you can do about this. The only influence you can have on this is to be the change you need to see. Do your part in reducing air pollution.

Ok, this might not solve anything anytime soon. If you live in an area which has poor air quality, and sometimes poor can be caused by naturally occurring disasters such as fires, you might consider simply training indoors. If you have air conditioning, you can ensure that you filter harmful toxins from the air. You might also consider bringing more plants into your home. Plants will filter the air and remove harmful toxins. You can buy air purifiers, I'm not sure they are necessary, and they don't look as nice as plants. If you're worried about maintenance, buy plants which are easy to look after, succulents are probably the easiest.

Alcohol (& drugs)

Hopefully you're not on illegal recreational or performance enhancing drugs, but, what about prescription medication. Speaking from personal experience, having been prescribed harsh mood-stabilising drugs for many years, I can personally tell you they are not helping you reach your goals. Even common anti-histamine pills might have a negative effect on your body's balance. Of course, there is a place to take medication, if your doctor has told you then who am I to tell you otherwise. You might want to get a second opinion, this might be from a holistic practitioner, or even from other people who are in your situation. In most cases you might not need the meds, I was told I'd never function without them and I'm doing fine now, many years after giving them up.

Unfortunately, again depending on where you are in the world, some doctors are offered incentives to prescribe medication. Completely unethical and you should really ask yourself whether the companies that research and manufacturer medication actually want you to get better, or if they really want you to be sick. After all, where would their business be if we were all perfectly healthy?

What do you do if you like a drink? If it's a lot and every day, maybe Alcoholics Anonymous… but, in all seriousness drinking is another influence your body has to deal with before recovering from your training. Ok, you might not want to give up alcohol completely, that's ok, everything in moderation and all that. But, maybe periodise your alcohol intake alongside your training. Get your fill of alcohol in the off-season when you're not competing and cut dramatically back, or even quit, during your racing season. If you find that hard, focus on allowing yourself to have a treat drink after your last race. Maybe stick a picture of your goals near where you keep your booze.

Recap

With all of the following items, consider your answer to the commitment questions when planning for this section.

1. Determine how much sleep you need per night and come up with a 'bed time' strategy to get high quality sleep.
2. Consider reducing some of the stressors in your life.
3. Consider a meditative or relaxation regime.
4. Consider your exposure to common sources of chemicals and whether you need to reduce or eliminate them.
5. Consider having a strategy for when air quality is low, if applicable.
6. Consider checking over your nutritional strategy, including alcohol intake.
7. If applicable, speak to a sports physician about any medication you are taking.
8. Ask yourself whether the decision you are about to make will reduce or increase the quality of your overall health.

Chapter Seventeen
Motivation

One of the biggest problems with motivation is that, once it disappears, it's hard to get it back. Preventative measures really are the best cure for lack of motivation. Everyone has drop-offs in motivation, usually induced by stress, poor performance, weather, or any other contributing factors, and I have some great tips to help you overcome this and stay the course throughout the year.

Visuals
First of all, at the start of your off-season, make a vision or dream board. This doesn't just have to be for cycling, it can be for the whole of your life. Write on it everything you want to achieve in the upcoming year. Times, places, points, categories, power outputs—literally anything. Use the SMART system outlined on chapter 3 *(page 28)* to create it. Your board needs to focus on a specific target (for example, winning your club championship) rather than just a vague aspiration. You need to aim for something that is measurable so that you will know for sure whether or not you achieved it. Make it challenging but achievable. Finally, you've got to target your goal to your own circumstances. To your board, add pictures, notes, and inspiration—in fact anything that comes to mind. Fill it up and then display it somewhere where you will see it often. Even better, you can announce it to the world which will help to keep you accountable. I display mine in my workroom, a place where my clients frequently visit me.

Display your best motivators in a prominent place so that you will see them often. I work with a lot of clients who overeat, or eat the wrong type of food. If they're not able to get rid of the food completely (for example, if they use a shared fridge) then they can display a picture in a prominent place to remind them why they are supposed to eat right. Many of my clients use a picture of me, pointing at them and frowning. They find that it works! Another idea is to find a picture of a trophy (or similar) and display it next to your trainer to inspire you to train. The most important thing is to identify your motivators as soon as possible because, if you leave it until you lose your motivation, you will not do it at all!

Depending on your reason why, you could start to add more motivational stimulus to your environment. Perhaps you need to start looking at pictures of your family on the walls of your home and associating that with success in your event. You can even use your family for this, next time you see your children, spouse or friends remind yourself of just how proud they will be when you succeed.

Musical/Vocal

You might find that music, imagery, prose or poetry is highly motivating to you. For example, you might find that playing your favourite music before an event or during a warm-up session, either through a pair of headphones or out loud, helps to get you in the zone. Think about what works for you at any point of the day, rather than just pre-race as this will help you to tune in to your body.

It doesn't stop at just music though. Do you have a favourite motivational speaker? If not, why not do a quick google search and see if there is anyone who inspires you. If you find one that you like, the mere sound of their voice might be enough to spark that excitement about your training.

You might also be someone who is self-motivating. Can you use an app like ThinkUp[li] to record some affirmations? Affirmations are short phrases that you repeat to yourself, sometimes this is vocally, sometimes this is read off a card to yourself, or in your head[lii]. This can be chanting or even simply shouting. Anything goes. The idea behind repeating the same phrase is that you start to manipulate your own psyche, you slowly start to change the way you operate in line with what is said in your affirmations. Sounds crazy? Is it going to hurt you to try this out? Write 10-25 affirmations on flash cards and read them to yourself once to twice per day. Do this for a month and see if you, or anyone close to you, has noticed a difference. They can be anything, not just athletic performance. It could be the way you want to behave, maybe you want a promotion or maybe you want to be less reactive in certain situations. A quick google search might help you really get to grips with this.

Smell/Taste

Think about the way in which you use each of the five senses and how one or more might spark associations in your mind that help with motivation. The smell or taste of something might fire you up. This might be the hardest to replicate, but, worth a mention.

Think of a time when you went into a grocery store, smelt the fresh baked bread and ended up motivated enough to buy some. Maybe this wasn't bread but bakery items or even barbeque food.

While it might have to be very obscure, if you are someone who really resonates with the olfactory senses, you might consider starting a regime to associate a certain smell or taste with your event. Perhaps you are training for a spring classic challenge, maybe it's the smell of Belgian waffles.

Ego

Everyone has one... while a lot of the time our egos seem complicit with our downfall, there is a strong argument for using your ego as a motivator. Of course, you need to be someone who responds to being competitive. This competitive spark, *you wanting to be the best*, might be exactly what you need to stay motivated.

Ask yourself how you'll feel if you fail? Maybe extend that to how you'll feel failing in front of everyone? Maybe take that one step further and ask yourself what other people will think or say about you? Use this as motivation to smash each session, eat right and be on task. Just ground yourself after doing this, once you have used your ego to complete a task, remind yourself that you will always give it your best and that your friends and family will support you regardless. You don't need to carry around the stress of failure, just use it at the appropriate times.

Just a final thought, if you've read this section and really don't think you relate, you're probably in the bracket of people with the biggest egos. Your ego is very good at making you believe you don't have one. Maybe you need a heart to heart with some close friends or family. Ask them honestly to tell you, are you egotistical, at all selfish or self-serving, or if you like to steer a conversation towards you. Just beware, if you are egotistical, you won't like the answer!

Recap
1. Decide what is the best means to keep yourself motivated. Do you prefer visuals, music, smell, taste or a combination?
2. Draw up a plan for what you will do when you find yourself lacking motivation.
3. Consider talking to a friend or family member that will check in with you and see how your training is going.

Chapter Eighteen
Time management

This is the amateur cycling enthusiasts' kryptonite! Time is usually the biggest limiter for anyone other than the professionals. You might have quite a bit of time if you no longer need to work, or your family is all grown up too, but, without being able to justify spending all your time focusing on athletic performance, you will need to find ways to maximise what you have available.

Event Demands

You'd be surprised how little time you need to train to actually reach most goals. For example, if you're training for an event that lasts for one hour, in general you will not need to train for more than one hour in any single session, so, if you have six hours free during the week, then that's plenty of time for your training!

If your event lasts 100 miles, you could identify your longest session in this way. Think about how long it'll take you to ride that 100 miles, you can reference some of your earlier training. This needs to take into account the terrain and conditions, but most importantly whether or not there will be opportunities to join a fast group. Make an estimate based on this and the answer you have is the absolute maximum you really need to do.

Of course, you can do more, if you have time. There is very little harm in that, providing you don't over-train and, in the case of you training for a one-day event, you're only doing more once per week. If you don't have time, you can take 70% of your duration and make this your desired training max for one session. It's worth noting that you still won't have to do this week in week out, simply having one session per week progressing towards this is enough.

Time Identity

As you can see, it's essential to identify the actual time you have available. You might think that you only have time to do half an hour's training a day. I'm sure this would be workable, but is it really all the time you have to spare? I wonder how much time you spend watching television, chatting on your phone or being on the internet. If you were really honest with yourself, you would no doubt find that you could easily turn that half hour into an hour.

It's only really multi-day events that you might consider needing a bit more time. Even then, it is perfectly possible to train for such an event on limited time, you just might be at a slight disadvantage to others.

First of all, start by identifying the priorities on your time. Write down all your essential daily activities such as sleeping, attending to matters of hygiene, eating and drinking, work commitments, time with your family, training, travelling — in fact, anything that generally fills your day. Next, determine which of these are your core or anchor activities — the ones that can't be moved, such as travelling and work commitments. Then identify those activities that can be reorganised in order to accommodate your training. For example, consider in what ways you might be able to compact certain activities so that you have a little more time available.

Perhaps you might be able to ask for a slight change to your working hours. Another consideration might be to combine activities, such as involving your family in your training programme such as core or leg strength work, or how you might be able to incorporate training into your working day, perhaps by commuting by bike, or by taking your bike to work so that you can use part of your lunch hour to train. In passing, as a coach, I think it's very difficult to get effective training into most commutes because the stop / start nature of the journey makes it difficult, although not impossible. In this respect, I'd use a commute for training as a last resort! Of course, if you like to commute and you told me that you want to do it and would sacrifice getting to your goals quicker to do it, I would make it work for you!

Time Fluidity

Maybe you've just read this chapter and thought 'doesn't apply to me', well that is awesome! What will you do with all your spare time? Well you might not want to just ride your bike more, just because you have the time to use, doesn't mean you should use it. After all, we want specific training, not over-training.

Have a think about what you have learned in this book. If you really identify with every aspect you could quite easily fill the gap where you'd be needlessly over-training with essential off-the-bike work, such as; optimising recovery, researching new and innovative equipment or training techniques (more on that in part four). How about meal preparation or even supporting your family more so they feel more inclined to support you when your race day comes.

ATP/TSS Mention

A quick word for those who aren't time strapped at all. In your case you should definitely look at planning your training around the most your body can recover from. A great indicator of this is previous data and a system such as Training Stress Score (TSS) as found in TrainingPeaks. Find your average TSS for a certain period of time, logically this is the previous season, but you might want to make a reasonable adjustment for any periods where you weren't able to meet a certain amount.

Be objective here. If you took a week off sick last year, you might not want to remove that from the average. Were you sick because you over-trained or was there another reason? Did you miss training due to something unforeseen? Did you achieve your goals, were you left feeling like you could've done more, or did you spend a lot of your time trying to recover? Did your recovery slow down much, or did it stay constant throughout the season? All these factors could indicate that you need to reasonably adjust how much TSS you train on average per week.

Once you have your figure, you can either go at it alone and allow progression each week, each block and with adequate recovery weeks, or, you can simply input this into the TrainingPeaks Annual Training Plan (ATP) feature.

Recap

1. Using your list of goals, consider how long your sessions need to be. Set a maximum and an average.
2. List all your time obligations. See which your anchors are, and which can be moved.
3. If you have a deficit and need to find time, consider combining activities together or finding ways to free up time.
4. If you have excess time, consider adding off-the-bike elements of this book into your day; meditating, meal prep and so on.
5. Also, if you have excess time, consider structuring your training around how much your body can cope with, rather than time available.

Chapter Nineteen
Pain management

Typically, cyclists appear to have a higher pain threshold than non-cyclists. I have no idea why this is, and I would welcome any evidence or studies that may have been carried out. It isn't very often that I have to spend a great deal of time with a client on pain management, but below I offer some ideas on how to achieve a higher pain threshold if this is what you need.

Train with Power
First of all, if you feel that pain is a problem for you, you might consider getting a power meter (if you haven't already got one) in order to see what sort of output you can achieve before your pain levels become unbearable. With a power meter, you should be able to work out some simple tests to help you identify what you should be able to do and then see how far off you actually are. This first step might actually solve the problem for you because you'll be more aware of what you should be able to do, and therefore more committed to actually achieving it. There is something oddly reassuring about knowing what your pacing is with a power meter, about knowing that you can definitely achieve a certain power output and knowing that all you have to do is push past the pain in order to achieve it.

Again, another really important tool at your disposal might be meditation. Train your brain to accept pain as part of this process and it will bother you less. It really will not hurt you to spend 10 minutes per day—this might be as part of your cool-down—meditating and increasing your mindfulness. Pain after all is just a feeling, we can learn to become accepting of these. Ever saw someone physically hurt themselves and not even flinch. Do you think they didn't feel it or that they are just accepting of its presence? While I'm not saying you'll be able to become superhuman with meditation, you will certainly find some benefits. Almost everyone who I have coached, and suggested meditation as a means to pain management, notes how they find an FTP test oddly easier...

Pain Barrier

It's one thing to know that you can push past a certain level of pain; it's another to know how to deal with the pain as you do so. Experience shows that, for many people, distraction tends to be an optimal method of dealing with pain. Of course, it's important to not distract yourself to the extent that you simply drop the power off in some sort of day dream. You need to be able to maintain a certain effort or power while not focusing on the pain.

Think about what you can see coming up in front of you, such as a tree at the side of the road, or a bend ahead. Tell yourself you are only racing until that point. When you reach that point, identify another point up ahead, and continue to repeat this exercise until you have completed the session. This method of pain control might sound simplistic, but it really works.

You might also use a cue sheet stuck to the top of your top tube. Most sportive events now have these as standard and they can provide a welcome count down for some people. Note, if you are not one of these people and rather like not knowing how long you have left of a certain effort, avoid placing the cues on your bike!

Think about the motivators you have identified in the previous chapter that might help, or 'power words' that you can repeat to yourself, either out loud or under your breath so that you don't waste too much energy! Find something that gets you pumped up!

There's nothing quite like scaring the crap out of someone as you ride past screaming. It's highly motivating, but take care not to be a nuisance, after all, I bet you have your name and number pinned to your back...

Warning Signs

Of course, it would be rather negligent of me to tell you to push through all pain, you need to be able to identify pain which can be conquered and pain which should be listened to. In most cases you can tell instantly which is which. The dull pain that tells you that you are working hard is something that can be used to pace well. As is that odd feeling in your body that you are at your limit, I don't liken it to pain at all, simply uncomfortable sensation that indicates I'm pushing hard.

Any sharp or sudden pain is something you should be listening to. Is it uneven, located in one place and are you struggling to engage that area of your body? Anything that really draws your attention should be considered.

I've been there. I trained for the best part of a year and rode 2000 miles across the United States, trying to set a World Record, only to be cruelly cut short with only 500 miles to go. I might have pushed on. I might have been able to spend an extra day in the saddle and taken more breaks. But, after a month rehabilitating my injury, I was able to start training again. Had I pushed on; I might not be able to ride at all now.

Be honest in these situations, are you doing more harm than good? Do you want to live to fight another day?

Don't make excuses, but don't be that guy who pushed through an injury and now needs extended recovery time.

Recap
1. Identify whether you feel you struggle with pushing through the pain, do you give up easily?
2. Consider introducing meditation into your day.
3. If you aren't already, consider buying a power meter so you can quantify your pain barriers.

4. Consider a strategy for dealing with pain; distraction, cue cards, power words.
5. Become more mindful of positive types of pain, ones that can be pushed. This will help you identify the ones that should be listened too.

Chapter Twenty
Breathing techniques

There is so much value in learning how to breathe properly, both on and off the bike. It will not only increase your endurance but also improve your speed. One study's results showed that you can 'increase your respiratory muscle endurance capacity by 12%. Performance on a bicycle time trial test designed to last about 40 min improved by 4.7%.' 'The results suggest that respiratory muscle endurance training improves cycling performance in fit, experienced cyclists.'[liii]

Fancy a shot at an additional 4.7%?

Take a moment to focus on your breathing habits, making sure your shoulders aren't hunched forward. Start breathing slowly and rhythmically through your nostrils as this is more effective at filtering and transporting oxygen to your lungs than mouth breathing. Make sure you send the breath all the way down to your stomach, expanding your abdomen and exercising the diaphragm and intercostal muscles.

Breathing deeply oxygenates your muscles so they can work harder, build strength and move faster. After you learn to breathe deeply, the challenge is to feel comfortable with the breathing rhythm that is optimal for the exercise you are doing.

Here is a perfect example:

1. Sit or lie flat in a comfortable position.
2. Put one hand on your belly just below your ribs and the other hand on your chest.
3. Take a deep breath in through your nose, and let your belly push your hand out.
4. Breathe out through pursed lips as if you were whistling.

5. Do this breathing 3 to 10 times.

Perfecting your breathing technique could be one of the key elements necessary to boost your all-round performance. Not that I like sounding like a broken record, but if you struggle with this then give meditation or yoga a go, efficiency in your breathing is one of the first things where you'll notice improvement.

Part Three – Recap
If you have followed this part correctly, you will now have:

1. Built a healthy living strategy.
2. Built a motivational strategy.
3. Identified and optimised your time needs.
4. Developed a strategy for dealing with pain.
5. Spent some time developing your breathing technique.

Congratulations! You are now three quarters of the way through this book and, if you implement your plan correctly, 100% closer (15% training, 35% nutrition and 50% mentality) to achieving your cycling goals! While this may sound like you are done, the final chapter focuses on ensuring that the intricate parts of the entire plan don't cause any upsets. After all, you don't want to spend the next nine months training and following all this advice, only to mess up in the final week.

Introduction

The following chapters might be considered 'the icing on the cake'. If you've worked through this book, you will have setup all your training and nutritional needs, and then complimented them with a thorough mental strategy. If you remember my formula for where your improvements come from; 50% Mentality, 35% Nutrition and 15% Training, then this section is a nice little bonus.

No doubt, if you do all the work you have set yourself in the previous chapters, you will have success in your goals. How smoothly it goes, and how effective you are, might be determined by compliance in one or more of the following areas. The final chapters may not even give you any performance benefit, but save you from making a mistake in the final hours. After all, why spend the next nine months training only to mess it up right at the end?

Here's an example, let's take our century rider we used at the start, they might spend thousands on a new bike, the most advanced equipment, use the latest technology and follow the best nutritional strategy suited to them, but if they get distracted in their warm-up and miss the start? They've blown it.

Perhaps this final section is more about not screwing up than it is gaining anything. Everyone has the potential to maximise the aerodynamics efficiency of their position, but, no one has unlimited potential. This section really is a level playing field, with the only limiter being how much you can, or are willing to spend. The arms race has gotten very intense with many people trying to shave weight from their bikes, cheat aerodynamic drag or supplement with some crazy untested product. This might prove difficult for you if you are on a tight budget. I will aim to give every budget a possibility in this last section.

You might be hoping that this section will be a comprehensive look at tactics for racing. If so, you may be a little disappointed because, by its nature, racing is dynamic and situational—even if you may know a huge amount about tactics, if you don't know who you are racing against your knowledge will invariably come to nothing. In this respect, rather than tactical expertise, the level of your experience will be an incredibly valuable asset to have and, in many cases, will allow you to think fast in order to create your own specific tactics or respond to the tactics others are using in a racing situation.

That said, there are areas of cycling in which a working knowledge of tactics is important, and, for that reason, the following tactical tips are offered for you to try. The main thing to take from any of the considerations below is to test them out prior to your most important events. Give them time, don't dismiss one instantly if it doesn't work out immediately and don't always expect perfect results, as there may be other things happening in your body or preparation that is causing an adverse effect. If you manage to achieve success with the tactical skills that I provide for my clients to consider, then you are doing well!

Chapter Twenty-One
Expertise Needs

Can you do this alone? Yes. Should you? Perhaps not! Let's face it, many of you will be willing to go out and spend thousands on new equipment to see a marginal gain, but, be reluctant to hire a professional to help with some other areas. What if I told you that, depending on your level you could see improvements of well over 30% with a coach, if you are very new you might even double your performance!

What about your new bike, wouldn't you like to be able to ride this comfortably, with no issues? A bike fitter here can resolve that! There are many different types of professional you can call in to give you a much-needed boost in performance. Some you might not need; some you should seriously consider. Here I try to give you an idea of what to expect from each and how to find a competent one.

Coach
I'm not biased when I say this, you should check what other people who have been coached say too, coaching is the most cost effective method of seeing improvements.[liv] Not only will a coach help you reach your goals and in many cases surpassing them, but, a good coach will also ensure that you learn more about yourself and how you should be training. A really good coach will teach you enough that, at some point, you don't need a coach to teach you anything else!

You might always consider being coached just for the accountability, that is why many coaches are coached themselves. It is all too easy to be biased with your own training. Wanting to go out and ride when you should be training indoors is a perfect example. For other cyclists, you might need to know someone is watching your training. Maybe you are someone who likes to impress, or maybe you don't like to look silly (not that you ever will!).

Either way, and depending on your current level, you should be expecting to see anywhere between 10-50% improvements with a coach. In reality, if you are either young or new to the sport, you could quite easily double your power output with a good coach.

Of course, I would love for you to become my client, or a client of any Spokes coach. However, I would settle for you to just be coached. Ensure that you do some research and find a coach that satisfies your needs. You should look for:

- A coach who specialises in your type of cycling.
- A coach with actual client testimonials and reviews.
- A coach with actual results.
- A coach who is fully qualified, vetted and insured.

Sadly, there are many people who have had a good experience themselves and think that makes them a good coach; it really might not. You wouldn't risk your home by hiring an unqualified contractor, would you? Why would you with your body! You get what you pay for. Try to go with the cheapest coach and you will get the cheapest service. Spend a little more, it'll still cost you less per year than that new wheelset or bike frame and it will give you far bigger improvements, while lasting longer too!

For those of you who say something like "I'm only targeting such and such event, I don't need a coach", really? You don't need to see significant improvements in your cycling? I always tell people that if I was looking to have a new house built from scratch, even if this was a really modest house, I wouldn't do it myself, I would hire a professional to do that. The same goes for cycling.

If you can't afford, or you're still not convinced you need to work one-to-one with a coach, you might look at a training plan.[iv] You can download some for free and you might start with a free plan, but, remember you're probably getting what you pay for; in this case not a lot. You still might double your chances of success with something 'off-the-shelf'. Try to get one tailored for your event, if this is the road you will go down.

Asides from working 1:1 with a coach, the most effective method is to engage with a coach to build you a personal plan. Many, many people find following a generic plan too difficult and then struggle to keep up or to progress forward. Others either fall behind or progress too quickly. Some people just don't see significant gains from a generic plan.

No matter what you do, try to make it personal. You should have training tailored to you. Truly Personal!

Bike Fitter
You can do all the training you want, but if you can't apply the power on the bike due to poor position then it will all go to waste. Similarly, the last thing you want is to get injured as a result of poor position. Simply put, nothing ruins a good bike like a bad fit. There should be no expectation that you should be in pain; you shouldn't have any discomfort or pain when riding so don't settle for anything less than comfort. For all these reasons and more, a good bike fit is worth every penny. Cheaper bike fits tend to be false economy. Buy well; buy once. A little more expense is usually a far quicker way to get results and you probably will get more for your money in terms of after-care.

Depending on your type of event, you will be looking at getting your bike into one of these three general fits:

Aero position
If you are racing, you're probably going to set your bike up to suit this position. It will be aggressive so you can reduce your considerable frontal drag, approximately 70% of all the drag occurs due to the rider. This might be slamming your front end or

if you are on a time trial bike, looking to really cheat the wind, while still applying the power.

Climbing position

If you are preparing for a hilly event, such as a sportive in the mountains, there will be times where aerodynamics plays a part but setting yourself up comfortably to climb will be more important than aerodynamics. You'll be holding the climbing position more throughout your event and the climbing positions tend to be kinder on your body and allow more oxygen into your lungs. Your position will be more upright, and your back angle will tend to be higher, with less pressure on your hands.

Comfort position

If you are riding an ultra-distance event, maybe an audax or even a tour, you will want to be as comfortable as possible. You are likely to be slower uphill or less aerodynamic, but you will be very kind to your body which will be far more beneficial than speed. Bear in mind the point might be to just finish, not to be the fastest, but, in most cases the most comfortable rider, or the one who stops the least, is the fastest one.

Much like coaching, you should do some research and find a fitter that will be most suited to your needs. Using your local bike shop might be a good start, but, unless they are carrying the latest technology, you could be visiting them a few times before you get it right. If you are going with someone who does their fitting with eye measurements and angles, you should try to ensure that you can come back as many times as you like for the one fee, until you get the fit spot on.

If you are looking to buy a new bike, the free fit you sometimes get with a bike purchase is a great start, but I'd recommend you spend more initially to get a great fit. Don't buy a bike and then get a fit; get a fit and then buy a bike. It will be worth it, and a good fitter will be able to recommend great frames to suit your body geometry.

I'm not sure anyone uses static bike fitting methods anymore; this is where you are motionless, and they fit you. A good bike fitter will have you pedalling on your bike so they can see you in action, this is called dynamic. You can take this one step further and employ systems such as Retul or Lemovo, both have had some excellent results, at a cost. Do your research and find a fitter that has results improving riders who are in the same discipline as you. Your friends and riding buddies will be a great resource for referrals.

There are very many systems that bike fitters use—from angular fits by eye, plumb bobs, protractors and other basic kit that a local shop might use, to the more efficient twenty thousand-pound jigs (such as trek precision fit or specialised body geometry) that professional fitters use. Many shops offer motion capture, which makes fitting to eye obsolete. Using video analysis is a faster way to a correct fit and will allow the fitter to replay little factors in your motion, showing you what they're looking at, whilst revealing key indicators, such as pressure mapping or knee misalignment. I'd recommend that you look for a fitter that doesn't use a single system but takes the best bits from different variations. Having someone not bound by the parameters of a single fit allows more flexibility and will bring more to the table, making for a better fit.

Top fitting centres will also carry pressure mapping systems which will quickly identify the points at which you are applying the most pressure, these will no doubt be the areas you experience pain, but then with a few adjustments of bike fit, see if the pressure has been reduced. An hour or so playing around with this might transform your riding.

It's also good practise to go see your bike fitter on a yearly basis. Your body will adapt, maybe you are increasing flexibility through core strength or yoga sessions, maybe you are just getting a little older and need a far less aggressive position. Either way, see your fitter each year which gives you the perfect opportunity to try some new kit like new shoes, new saddles, new anything!

If you are into time trial, look at seeing a bike fitter who specialises in this area. A great bike fitter might have access to a velodrome or wind tunnel that, while expensive, will be a short cut to finding a wind cheating position. This is where you will see the biggest performance increase, and this might be the only factor I might suggest you do before hiring a coach.

Once you have your correct fit, set up a mirror next to your trainer and train in front of it until you are able to perfectly hold the desired position for an extended period of time. Practising being on the drops isn't just for those who time trial, it's also great for any racing or event preparation. Aerodynamics is an area in which you can see big gains.

What to do if you are on a real tight budget? First of all, you'll need to learn the basics of bike fitting, get online and find some blogs about it, especially with diagrams depicting what ideal position might look like. Then get someone to video you on your bike, indoors on a trainer. Using software such as Dartfish[lvi] or Coach's Eye[lvii], you can start to work your position into the desired one.

You might need to do a lot of fiddling and self-diagnostics. Slight twinges are warning signs that your position is not quite right. A big warning here, you might spend much time perfecting this and in reality, it might take you years to achieve what a professional bike fitter could do in a few hours.

Genealogist

Ok, sounds expensive, but it doesn't have to be. Some coaches now specialise using systems such as Fitness Genes, the system we use at Spokes. As it sounds, this is DNA based data. You get a kit in the mail, put some saliva in it and return it and within a couple of weeks you have a whole mass of data which gives you potential markers for certain depositions.

Factors such as whether your body runs better on carbohydrates or fats, if there are any likely intolerances, whether you are sensitive to certain foods, alcohol or caffeine. From a performance perspective, how fast your body will recover, whether your genes suggest you are suited to intense power training or steadier aerobic training.

Armed with all this info you can really tailor your training to your exact needs. If anything, I recommend this type of test solely to find out what nutritional strategy you employ. The tests are relatively inexpensive too, a couple of hundred pounds/dollars at most.

Nutritionist

While there are free online resources, such as my Nutritionally Fit programme, you might consider hiring a nutritionist to help you make the most of that 35% improvement this could bring.

If you are considering hiring a nutritionist, ensure you find one who is constantly updating their qualifications. The world of nutrition changes very rapidly, one who hasn't updated their knowledge recently might be practising outdated theories.

You might see a nutritionist as necessary if you suffer with any digestive problems or have a lot of intolerances or allergies. A good nutritionist will no doubt be a massive time saver and help you greatly. While a nutritionist will bring you a whole host of benefits, if you are on a budget, you might look to spend your money elsewhere.

Sports Psychologist / Mental Fitness

Big in the professional world, it is very rare that I meet an amateur athlete who has hired a sports psychologist. I predict we will see this increasing over the next few years as athletes look to unleash more of their potential through brain training. If 1:1 mental fitness coaching could become more cost appealing, I think we would see more immediately, for now, most people are happy looking for good books or using apps such as Headspace or Think-Up to get ahead of the competition.[lviii]

Given I place around 50% of your improvement in this area, how much would you be willing to part with? There are plenty of courses you can take[lix], if you're on a budget.

Sports Physician

Another area we don't really see many athletes pursuing. In reality, this is probably something that is niche to professionals, especially in countries like the United Kingdom with free health care. Albeit your local GP might not be the best person to diagnose a sporting injury, they might refer you to someone who could. It is unlikely that your medical insurance will cover any sports related issues, so you might be left to foot the bill here, this could be the reason amateur athletes don't bother.

From a personal experience, I would recommend a sports physician if your targets are somewhat dangerous to your health. By this I mean you are competing in an event with a high chance of injury. Ultra-endurance events are such. Repeated rides day-in-day out are a breeding ground for injury and preventative efforts such as seeing a qualified sports physician might be what you need to get through.

Recap

1. Using the demands of your event, list your desired expertise needs.
2. Workout your budget and see exactly where you could see the biggest gains for your money.
3. Before you spend anything, complete the following chapter.

Chapter Twenty-Two
Equipment Needs

First of all, if you don't already have a bike and are planning to enter a cycling event, you might want to go and get one! Lance Armstrong stated that 'it's not about the bike', it's actually the title of his book, but had Lance not been able to afford a bike it might be a different story. Sean Yates had a different perspective naming his book 'it's all about the bike', although you can read into that if you will.[ix]

Regardless of how much you can attribute your success to your equipment, if you have money to spare, you might consider investing in one or more of the following. Read this entire part first to ensure you make the most of your investment. If you have the money, I won't shame you for following all these suggestions, what I will do though, is trying to pick out the most important ones, so that if you are on a budget, this part won't completely alienate you.

Bike
Do you need the best bike? No. In fact, some of the world's best pro teams don't use their top range bikes, and if they do, some might be weighed down to conform to strict weight limits. If you have the money a top of the range bike might make the difference, but, a moderately priced bike with mid-range components, such as Shimano Ultegra, is good enough for most situations.

If you are competing, or you have money to spare, then doing a little bit of research and finding the best bike for your discipline might give you an edge. The difference between a base time trial bike and the top range one, could be significant over a 25-mile TT. A lightweight frame might make a big difference to someone who is targeting hillier events. Take a look at some of the bikes used at Hill Climb events, most you wouldn't ride around on; just uphill a few times a year!

Only you can decide whether you need to upgrade your bike. Factors including the spec, and perhaps state, of your current bike, what your targets are and your budget, plus many more, will help you decide. Look back over the notes you've compiled completing this book, have a look at what your competitors ride. If you are planning to step into time trial or are reading this to level up on the cycling leg in triathlon, then moving from a standard road bike to a TT/Tri bike is a massive step in the right direction.

For those who aren't competing, what do others ride who do your event? If you're riding an old shopping bike with three gears and you want to take on an Alpine event with several thousand meters of climbing, an upgrade might be necessary. Although I have a lot of respect for those who place themselves at an obvious disadvantage by using a bike not suited to the event; fixed gear for an ultra-event, or folding bike to climb Mont Ventoux.

The difference between entry level bike spec and mid-range (for example the difference between Shimano 105 & Ultegra) is much bigger than the difference between mid-range and top spec. If you are new to cycling or upgrading from a very basic setup, I strongly recommend trying to make the mid-range work, you get so much more for your money than at any of the other levels.

Wheels
Once you have a decent frame, even if it has entry level components, such as Shimano 105, you might find the biggest improvement you can make is with a set of wheels. Again, think very carefully about what you are targeting. A nice set of deep-section carbon wheels sounds great, until you get pummelled around in the wind and no-one wants to ride near you. Similarly, those heavier deep-sections might not be the best for going uphill and before you go out and buy the lightest set, consider where you have to ride these, most sub-kilogram wheelsets are designed for flawless road surfaces, one pothole might buckle a rim.

Again, it's not entirely necessary to get the best wheels, but, a good pair of wheels might make more of a difference than a new frame. Carbon wheelsets have had some reported issues in the past, particularly under heavy, repeated braking, or braking in the wet, but, if you've got disc brakes you don't need to worry. The cost-conscious cyclist, with rim brakes, might get carbon wheels with alloy braking surface.

If you are already on a mid-range bike setup, I recommend spending more money on a wheelset upgrade, you will certainly see more speed doing this. If you are on an entry level setup and considering upgrading your bike, you could see if your local bike shop can do you a deal on both. Most mid-range bikes come with very basic wheels as manufacturers know that they'll either get upgraded or a customer will have their own set already.

Your bike has to be very basic for me to believe your money would be better spent on frame/new bike rather than new wheels.

Power Meter
In so many ways, a power meter will probably give you the biggest improvements for your money. Not only will it allow you to train in a more structured manner, but it will help you understand how to better pace and give you far more data to improve your training.

They aren't as expensive as they once were, but, do some research and don't buy the cheapest. See what others have experienced; did many people end up returning them, were there complaints about accuracy or reliability? Any of these issues can make training with power complicated and frustrating.

While there are many places you can install a power meter, I strongly recommend looking at a pedal-based system. Unless you are flush with money and can buy a power meter for each bike you own, a pedal-based system will make swapping between bikes much easier.

Most models also come in two options, dual sided (where the power is measured on both sides – how it does that can be quite different though!) or single sided (where the power is measured on one side then doubled). If you have the money, a good dual sided power meter will give you a better look at what you pedal efficiency is like. Are you pedalling stronger with one leg, do you fatigue in a ride and then lose power through either side? If you are on a budget, single sided power meters are just fine too.

If you can't, or don't want to, upgrade to using a power meter right now, then you should at least be using heart rate. If you don't already have a heart rate monitor, get one, they are very inexpensive and will make your training so much more effective.

Groupset
Here we are talking about the components your bike has. There are three main options; Shimano, Campagnolo and Sram, with many less conventional ones as well. Depending on what you currently have, you might not experience much more performance from your bike by upgrading here, maybe a slight weight benefit aiding climbing.

What you will experience is greater ride experience. Shifting will be better and this could add speed if your current setup is preventing you from shifting cleanly. You might also consider an electronic version of your groupset. While I don't think these are necessary on road bikes, should you be time trialling, the advantage to having buttons instead of levers both makes crucial gear changing easier and cheats the wind more effectively.

When buying a new bike, primarily the difference in price simply comes in the spec of the groupset. If you are in need of a total overhaul, then buy everything together. The difference between entry to mid-range then mid-range to top has the same problem occurring here; you get far more value upgrading from entry to mid-range than you do mid-range to top.

I know many people, myself included, who prefer to simply buy a new bike with top spec and then, as the parts wear down, replace it with mid-range. It is far more cost effective and the difference isn't always worth the additional expense.

The only exception might be if you plan to race. If you are building a lightweight bike, you might not upgrade the groupset at all, simply some of the parts of it. If you are racing at a high level, or simply have the money, then the shifting and weight saving of top spec will be an advantage.

If you are on a budget, I simply do not recommend upgrading here, look to get gains elsewhere or save your money and upgrade the entire bike. Maybe the exception is if you have a frame you really like, or perhaps your bike is vintage.

Components
There might be no reason why you'd need to upgrade any components of your bike, saddle perhaps the exception which I will go through below. Items such as handlebars, stem, bar tape, quick release skewers, bottle cages and pedals are all places where one might look to save weight or increase comfort.

If you are reducing weight, shop around to find the lightest parts, however, you might have to spend some big money to see significant gains in some of these areas! Quick release skewers are one that always surprises people, relatively inexpensive to reduce quite a bit of weight over standard ones.

If you are looking to add comfort, you might consider a double wrap of bar tape. This will reduce impact on your hands. Ensure you test everything before heading for your main event.

Of course, you can upgrade any part of your groupset too, although it might be entirely unnecessary, again, the main reasons would be as you can save weight in some areas or that you had worn your previous part out.

Saddle

Get one that suits you! Simple really, if you don't find the one you are on comfortable, then try something else. It might take a while, but you will find the right one eventually. Go to a decent bike shop, one that offers free trials and has a bike fitting centre, preferably with a pressure mapping kit, this will reduce the time it takes to find your perfect saddle.

You will also need to consider your shorts, the chamois and then some chamois cream. These three areas can be the culprit. If you have ill-fitting shorts, the pad might move causing friction, it simply could be a pad size that doesn't work for you, and you could try reducing friction using a cream. If the pain in your area occurs less than an hour into your ride, it is almost certainly the saddle. If it is longer than an hour, then it is something else; such as sweat causing swelling of the pad or lycra.

If you are really suffering, try the Infinity Bike Seat[lxi] or a Brooks[lxii], game changer for me and my super sensitive seat area!

Regardless of your budget, if you are having issues in this area you will need to sort this out as a priority. Not only will this improve your ride experience, but, if you are constantly moving around, having to stand up or fidgeting, you will be lacking performance too.

Helmet

These next two categories might have the biggest gains for your money. An aero helmet, time trial specific if you are racing (do not go time trial specific if you are just riding around though!), might shave 10-20 seconds from an all-out hour effort over 25 miles. Depending on your current setup, this might be the biggest gain you will see, except for the next category. It is certainly the most cost-effective. At no more than a few hundred pounds/dollars this is one of the largest amounts of improvement per £/$ spent you'll find.

On the opposite side of this, on a hot day, you will need a helmet that allows as much heat as possible to leave your head. I go through my 'Hot Weather Training' specifics in chapter 24 *(page 198)*, but even a small amount of overheating will cause a huge amount of drop off in performance.

Upgrading here will be dependent on your event demands and current model. If you are riding a flatter route, where speed will be crucial, then an aero lid will be better than a standard version. If you will be riding in hot climates, then ensuring you have got adequate ventilation is a must.

Clothing
Here is where you can see substantial improvements. A skinsuit might save you 20-30 seconds over an hour effort covering about 25 miles. For the cost, maybe a few hundred pounds/dollars, you might not find any better cost-efficient speed improvements, from equipment at least.

Of course, like helmets, you need to consider your environment. If it is going to be hot, you stand to lose more performance through overheating than you will gain through being more aerodynamic. Most skinsuits also don't have pockets, this might be an issue if you are riding a longer event and need to bring food.

If you are on a budget, or if you don't want to wear a skinsuit, upgrading from your looser kit to a more race cut will make a big difference. Bottom line is it should also be comfortable.

Shoes
As long as you have carbon soles, the main focus on shoes will be comfort. If you start to get foot pain, or 'hot foot', you will really

struggle to continuously apply the power, you might even need to stop to relieve the pain. If you are going to be riding in hot conditions, you should check that your feet will be ok in your current shoes. Training indoors, with the fan off, is a great way to do this as it will cause your feet to expand and immediately identify whether you have enough room in your shoes.

You can get some serious aerodynamic gains from shoes too, if this is a need for you. You might also use shoe covers if they don't cause your feet to overheat. There are various methods of tightening the shoes, some more adjustable on the move than others. Again, look at what your event demands are, do you need comfort or speed. If the answer is neither, you should be fine with your current ones.

However, if you can afford it, you might consider two pairs of shoes. One slightly larger which you can use in hot climates. It also doesn't hurt to have a backup; the closing ratchets can break, and it would be an issue if this were to happen right before your main event. You won't need to spend a lot of money.

Recap
1. List your current equipment spec.
2. Using the demands of your event, list your desired equipment spec.
3. Workout your budget and see exactly where you could see the biggest gains for your money, ensure you also include your reasoning in the previous chapter.

Chapter Twenty-Three
Tactics for training and racing

When you're training, are you setting yourself up for success, or failure? The following nuggets of info might come in use for you as you look to perfect a routine which ultimately allows you to make the most out of every session. Like I mentioned in the introduction to this part, you might only see improvements from these, if you're not considering them already. Anyone can utilise these factors to their benefit and they are not limited by any outside factor, such as potential of your financial position.

If you're looking for advice on racing tactics, I'd suggest you speak to members of your team, club or a local coach who will be able to guide you through their thoughts on how you, personally, should approach a specific race as opposed to attempting to consider imaginary scenarios. There's no book that will replace the knowledge and experience of a good Team Manager, Ride Captain or Directeur Sportif. These people have learnt to read a race. They can adapt a plan accordingly, sense who is suffering and who is feeling good. They will be able to dictate and make decisions on the fly. They are invaluable. Regardless of what level you are at, if you don't have one of these people in your team or at your disposal, make friends with one.

Of course, you might not be racing at all, but you might still find help in people who have ridden your target event before. Even experienced Gran Fondo or Sportive riders will be able to give you valuable advice on the course, the preparation of the event organisers or the officials. Search them out and ask their advice, almost all of them will be honoured you thought to approach them.

Warm-up
I've had an incredible number of testers (cyclists specialising in time trials) come on board and get a personal best on their first week due to my asking them to focus on a different warm-up. In

my opinion, British Cycling has the perfect warm-up (WU) for you
to start with, as follows:

- 5 minutes cadence 90
- 2 minutes cadence 95
- 2 minutes cadence 100
- 2 minutes cadence 105
- 1 ½ minutes cadence 110
- 30 seconds cadence 120
- 2 minutes cadence 90
- 6 seconds sprint
- 1 minute cadence 90
- 6 seconds sprint,
- 1 minute cadence 90
- 6 seconds sprint
- 2 minutes 42 seconds cadence 90

Learn it and do the whole thing before any of your high intensity
key sessions or time trials, in fact before any session that requires a
thorough warm-up. You'll soon memorise the warm-up, then all
you need to do is make to subtle changes to it until you find
something that works 100% of the time. You might want to add
some dynamic stretching which helps engage more muscle groups
than those that are worked during cycling, such as:

- Squats
- Lunges
- Side leg raises
- Bridges

You could also add any movement to awaken a part of your body
that might be sore or at an injury risk, for example, if you have
sore calves, maybe do some calf raises.

A good warm-up doesn't just get your body ready; it'll help to focus you mentally. It's for this reason that I ask clients to get into a routine. You need to prepare for the task you're about to undertake so chatting with your mates, messing about or being distracted in any way shouldn't be a part of it. Use the warm-up time to fill your mind with positivity. For example, you could meditate or be mindful about how your body is feeling. Racing with a positive attitude produces positive results; unfortunately, the same goes for a negative attitude. You can factor in some of your motivational routine into your WU, maybe play some loud music, chant your power words, or read through your affirmations.

You may also want to develop a shorter warm-up routine for other events or training. For example, there's not really any need to do a twenty-minute warm-up for a base endurance ride at low intensity. Similarly, you need to develop one for the turbo and one for the road. Practically speaking, you can't always take a turbo with you prior to a sportive but having something you can do for the first ten minutes to get your body and mind ready is better than hammering out of the gates and sustaining an injury.

Having the ability to conduct a warm-up on the turbo or on the road will help should you find that a turbo is not allowed in the car park of your venue. All you need to do is to plan for every possibility which will reduce stress on the day should something not go to your normal plan. You might even go so far as to have one for different events. Time trials are a perfect example since most people will warm up in a different way for a hill climb or ten-mile TT than they would for a 12 or 24-hour. This is worth consideration if you do a lot of different disciplines.

Warm-down
Although it's considered a little unconventional nowadays, I refer to the warm-down as a 'cool-down'. The main focus of a cool-down is to kick-start the recovery process so you should focus on this when developing yours. For this reason, the only way you'll be

able to tell if it's working is by how you feel after the session and over the next few days. This might prove to be a little confusing, as you'll need a reference point and also need to factor in training and fitness, but it is entirely possible.

A perfect start to a cool-down is simply 10-20 minutes of light pedalling in an easy gear, high cadence with a low power or effort. Then 10-20 minutes of further stretching, perhaps with your foam roller. You might practice some mindfulness in your cool-down, allowing your body to focus on the areas that need to recover. Do all of this whilst replenishing lost fluids and carbohydrates alongside regulating your core temperature, which in almost all cases involves putting a hoodie or other layers on even when you are feeling warm. Again, this is something for you to take away and develop.

Fuelling (training)
The main principles of fuelling are covered in detail in Part Two. However, there are some key points that pertain specifically to tactics that will help you to improve your tactical skills. First of all, consider that training provides the perfect opportunity to learn exactly what works best for you. There are some general rules that will apply to most people, but instead of listing them I am going to encourage you to test, test, test! It's important not to listen to your best mate, for example, who swears by fast food and alcohol (or anything slightly less exaggerated!). Make notes as you test and, just as described elsewhere, try something at least a couple of times before either adopting it as a win or binning it as a loss. One thing I am a fan of is the 'train low, race high' principle. This means eating less when you are training in order to get the body to fuel more efficiently from its own stores and then to eat more when you are racing in order to optimise the amount of fuel the body is utilising. Typically, this means that your body will have more than enough to work with. Again, the amount of fuel you need is something to think about and experiment with in order to discern the best results for you as an individual. A word of warning; under

fuelling throughout training will risk poor quality sessions and introduce too much fatigue which you'll no doubt carry through into the racing season.

Fuelling (racing)

If you are fuelling your training correctly, you will have a good idea about what works and what doesn't. The best advice is not to change the formula on your event day! Many people have found that trying a different breakfast, a gel, bar, or a drink can ruin a race or event. Just trust that you've done the right thing so far and stick with it. If you've also trained slightly 'low' in the way suggested above, then plan to eat a little more. Again, this is something worth testing at C or even B events but eating more will generally help your body to perform better. I always recommend starting on solid food like bars or homemade flapjacks, then moving on to more liquid sources later. This is because it's likely you will crave the instant sugar more if you start on gels, then if you go back to bars it won't have the same effect and might make you feel nauseous. As mentioned already, another piece of advice to note is not to trust feed station food. It might look nice and it might taste nice, but I bet it's been sitting there all day, and I bet it hasn't been refrigerated. Watch as people paw their way through food, dripping sweat on it, or insects stop by to feast on it. Do you really want that in your body just at the moment when you are wanting to perform at your best?

Fuelling (timing)

Here's a base guide to get you started with when and how often you should be ingesting some form of fuel:

- Before (two to three hours out): A normal meal, conforming to your nutritional strategy.
- Before (thirty minutes to one hour): Black coffee (unless you are sensitive to caffeine), small piece of fruit. No fats nor protein.

- During: Any session lasting less than one hour in duration: Nothing.
- During: Any session indoors lasting less than 2 hours: Homemade electrolyte drink only – unless this is a key session at high intensity, at which point you might consider fuelling as per your race day plan.
- During: Any ride outdoors lasting 2 hours: Maximum intake should be one homemade bar and one homemade electrolyte or energy drink. If this is low intensity nothing. Again, if this is a key session at high intensity, you may consider fuelling as per your race day strategy.
- During: Any ride/session lasting more than 2 hours: You should aim to consume around 250 calories per hour. Ideally this will be made up of homemade bars and/or homemade energy drinks. Your body cannot digest more than around this amount so do not eat more. If low intensity just your homemade electrolyte drink (take a bar just in case).
- After all sessions: If you are not eating within 30-45 minutes of the end of your session then a recovery drink is ideal. Protein only needs to be added here if you are significantly under your protein intake for the day (this might be in the case of fasted or long rides).

THE BEST ADVICE YOU WILL EVER READ: Test this out, it is not a perfect solution, not everyone will find this works, in particular test the foods you are eating!

Fuelling (examples)
Because I've mentioned homemade a few times now...

Homemade Flapjacks:
Makes 10 squares (10 portions)
300g rolled oats

50g chopped nuts – any you like (Brazil nuts, almonds, walnuts, cashews etc)
50g seeds – any you like (pumpkin, sunflower, chia, flax seeds etc)
100g dried fruit – any you like (raisins, sultanas, apricots, figs etc)
1 tsp cinnamon
1 tsp salt
500ml dairy free alternative to milk
1 medium egg
1 tsp vanilla extract
Preheat oven to 175C or gas mark 4. Mix dry ingredients. Mix wet ingredients. Pour wet into dry. Stir to combine. Pour into a 9 x 9 baking dish either coated in a little coconut oil or lined with parchment paper. Bake for 20-30 minutes. When cool, cut into 10 squares.

Homemade Energy Drink:
This is simple... one-part organic, locally sourced apple juice (no added sugar!), one-part water, small pinch of salt.

Homemade Electrolyte Drink:
This is even simpler... water, small pinch of salt. Add more salt if you cramp or in hot temperatures.

The money I've just saved you, potentially thousands per year, by helping you not buy cheaply manufactured sports products can be put towards the list you've created above. You're welcome.

Activation Routine

Some people will use the term 'activation' in reference to their warm-up, maybe terming it as the bit where they stretch to activate the body. However, I use the term as the routine riders do to activate their minds and body the day before a big event.

Start by developing your 'day-before routine' the day before your testing or C events. This won't disrupt your training too much and, in my opinion, the gains from getting your preparation right far outweigh any potential training gains. It won't hurt you, but, getting this nailed so it gives you that little boost the next day is well worth it for your main targets.

Next, you need to consider what your activation actually consists of. You need to develop a 'day before' session that will help your body to feel ready for the race day itself. In my experience, many racers do too much and many who train recreationally or for sportives do too little, or, even worse, nothing at all. There are a few people who say they have done enough testing and that they race better after a day of complete rest. My belief is that there are other factors that are impacting their performance. For example, they may have over-trained and therefore the rest day is actually allowing their body to have a period of recovery which may provide them with a mild boost on the race day itself.

Start your activation by doing your warm-up. An effective warm-up will prepare you mentally and help you get in the zone. After your warm-up, take some time to work at the expected pace for your race event the following day. Bear in mind that, if you are riding a 100-mile sportive at an easy pace, then this will be at a slower pace than if you are riding a time trial at threshold. Next, do your event warm-down (or cool-down), as outlined above. These tactics are your template. Now all you need to do is test this template before your C events or testing, ensuring you make relevant notes on how you feel, and make subtle changes until you get it 100%, or as close as you think you'll ever get. In reality, you might always be looking to develop this a little more, squeezing anything from it costs you nothing and might give you a percent or two extra in performance.

The timing of your preparatory session will make the world of difference. Some people prefer to leave it quite late in the day, which is fine if it works for them. I prefer clients to start at roughly the same time as the event the next day as this will help them get in the zone for the race itself. The exception to this might be if you are racing very early in the morning as you may consider the extra rest more beneficial.

The remainder of your preparation includes, but is not limited to, hydrating, fuelling, resting, getting your feet up, reducing stress through meditation or mindfulness, final course or route preparation, possibly watching a video of a previous race if there's one available and, finally, setting your alarm and having an early night. You might think you should include final checking of gear in your preparatory list, but I would highly recommend that you should check your gear at least a week in advance in order to find, and rectify, any possible problems.

Tapering

All your hard work will go to waste if you don't allow your body to adapt to the training leading into your A events. For this reason, athletes have been using tapering tactics for years. The general principle of a taper period is to allow the body to fully recover from training stimulus without losing any form, which is what could happen if you were to take a couple of weeks off. For most people, a taper will last between 10 and 14 days, but I know of riders who take more time than this, and I know of at least one rider who won't taper at all, but this isn't something I'd recommend. Two weeks tends to be the most popular time simply because, on average, that is how long it takes for the adaptation to fully take place in your body. Again, you and your coach could practice and test this to determine a more accurate reflection. You can design a taper to suit your individual needs but there are three main types of taper, generally called step, linear and exponential.

A step taper involves a quick reduction in load (volume or intensity, or combination of both) starting from day one. A step taper would look like a horizontal line. A linear taper is a gradual reduction in load, again of volume, intensity or a combination of both, whereby you could draw a straight line on a graph with a linear decline from day one through to the event day. Lastly, the exponential taper, which is the most commonly used, involves a dramatic reduction in the volume of training without it being a complete drop-off. The decline is steeper than the linear taper and smoother than the step taper. An alternative fourth taper utilises a curved line where you see a steep drop off at the beginning which then flattens out approximately at the half way point. (See model below)

Whichever type of taper you utilise, the most common method is to reduce volume very quickly whilst retaining intensity. This tends to promote recovery without loss of performance. Whichever taper you use; you should test your tapers out by including easier or recovery weeks in your plan. Three optimum peaks (three A events) is commonly the most you'd see in a season. When testing, factor in that you won't taper for two full weeks until you are actually preparing for an A event. In this way you will gain an understanding of the benefits of tapering and you should feel better and perform stronger having had a full taper prior to your A event. Whatever you do, aim to achieve approximately a 6% increase in power outputs, which is commonly held to be the latest calculated figure on recognised gains through an efficient taper.[lxiii]

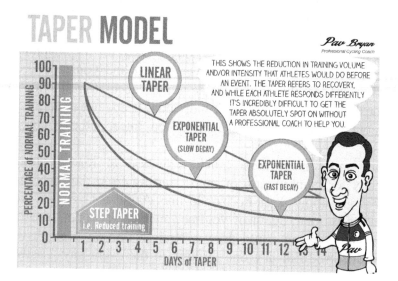

Pacing

Even the hardiest of veteran racers gets pacing wrong, from time to time, and even the ever-increasing popularity of power meters won't prevent incorrect pacing occurring at some point. If you have a power meter, then pacing does become considerably easier. If you use a heart rate monitor, you'll need to be pretty good at recognising when your heart rate isn't providing an accurate reflection, for example, due to nerves before a big event or lack of sleep. I'd recommend that you spend time learning how to listen to your body in order to glean vital clues about your event day performance and whether or not you'll be able to sustain a particular effort. Arguably, the most efficient pace would resemble a perfectly flat power line from start to finish. This would be great if there were no variables such as wind, temperature, fatigue, time, terrain and so on!

I know many riders who practice the method of 'hard-easy-hard'. The idea behind this is that it is likely that, mentally, you will have a harder time in the middle of the race and then a burst of motivation to finish strong. Therefore, it actually pays to go out harder, recover slightly in the middle and push at the end. This seems to work for some people and is worth a try if you've not experimented already with this pacing tactic. Giving it a go at your club's local 10-mile time trial would be an excellent time to try it out. Hills and wind are the two biggest problem-causing factors. The majority of cyclists will benefit from pushing a little harder into both the wind and up hills. The reason for this is that, inevitably, there is usually a tail wind or descent to come later, at which point holding a higher amount of power can be problematic and recovering from a harder effort beforehand becomes logical. This is where your preparation comes in, because you'll know where the course has harder sections and where you will be able to recover. Keep an eye on the weather forecast and plan your attack for the wind factor. Check out whether or not your course runs along a main road. If it does, cars provide a much-needed pull as they pass and they can provide protection from the wind, but it's no good expecting them to be there.

Competition
Competition tactics are aimed mainly at those who ride time trials, although some of this information will apply equally to those riding recreationally or in sportives. The following tips are usually picked up automatically, simply through experience, but if you've not considered them, they'll provide a welcome head start!

First of all, race your own race. Don't get sucked into a race you can't win, don't try to beat someone better than you, don't get over-confident and don't let the moment compromise all the hard work you've put into training. You should know your limits from the training and preparation you have done.

Secondly, don't deviate from your plan. There are far too many riders who train all year knowing exactly what power they can sustain for a race only to go out and blow it in the first few miles believing that today will be their day and that they'll somehow get race-day super human powers! Of course, you will want to factor in certain aspects, such as knowing that you may output more power on the road than you do indoors, and you might have added motivation and determination during a race. However, you should be able to work this out in your C or even B events in order to not go into your A events using guesswork alone. It is best to have a plan and stick to it, unless you are road racing, in which case your plan might need to change depending on the situation.

Thirdly, for those who ride recreationally in a group, and for those who ride sportives, you might have to put an added effort in to keep up, but, if you're successful and skilled enough to ride comfortably in a group then the savings in effort will be considerable. Depending on your place in the group, your ability and the wind conditions, you can expect to save 50% energy compared with riding solo (or being at the front).[lxiv] So it might be hard work to hang on but you will be doing considerably better than you would if you were riding solo. However, you should know your limits. A power meter will help immeasurably as you will be able to see whether or not you are holding your pace for the duration.

A final point to bear in mind is that it's unlikely the group will take much pity on you if you are unable have a turn at the front through being too exhausted and, similarly, if the group is simply too strong you don't want to be in a situation where they spit you out the back so that you are on your own and you have burnt all the matches in your pack!

Recap
1. Commit to learning your warm-up and warm-down routine, adapting this in every meaningful session until you've mastered it and created one that works 100% of the time (note: this might be something you are always looking to slightly adapt).
2. Using your nutritional strategy from Part Two, note down your ideal training and racing fuelling plan. Commit to adapting this, again it might take years too perfect and might always need changing every time you change your nutritional programme.
3. Pencil in your calendar ideal times to test activation sessions and your taper. Both will be before testing and C events. You will not need to do a full taper, just something to see what your body responds well too. You can then try a longer taper before your B events. Commit to adapting this until you find the perfect one (again, don't be surprised if this takes a few years to get 100%).
4. Commit to becoming a pacing master. Even if you don't plan to race in the future, local time trials offer an excellent opportunity to get pacing perfected.

Chapter Twenty-Four
Hot Weather Training

Something that has been talked about, but never given much credit is training in heat. Think about training at altitude, how much that is revered. The following is the culmination of over a year's study and work, resulting in the guidelines for my hot weather training methodology.

Think of a time you have been for a ride in heat, maybe this was a trip abroad or a sudden change in temperature at home, maybe this was even your target event. Did you perform as well at that temperature as you had been while training? Were there any issues with hydrating or keeping cool? Perhaps you had to take longer to recover after? These are all real issues that I have experienced as both and athlete and a coach.

A chance meeting through social media, and then in person, between myself and Spruzza President and Inventor, David Carrozza while I was visiting my partner some 5000 miles away from my home was what sparked my curiosity with thermodynamics[lxv]. This led to the joint creation of this methodology and the protocol that built the training plan which has been tested by many athletes including professional cyclist Evan Huffman.

The goal of the Hot Weather Training Methodology is to:

- Increase awareness and appreciation for the effect hot weather has on training, racing and the body.
- Explore both historical and innovative approaches to helping athletes train in the heat.
- Help athletes to self-assess their individual heat tolerances, experiences as well as existing health conditions that impact heat tolerance.

- Prepare athletes with the right steps and gear to maximize the experience and results when they can't avoid the heat.

This and what follows in the Spokes Hot Weather Training Methodology is designed to provide some basic, and some detailed, explanations on why beating the heat is smart no matter how tough you are. No matter what your summer riding goals are having the ability to stay cooler improves the experience and the memory.

Whether you are training to compete on the World Tour, complete a Gran Fondo or simply to better yourself, we are going to help you accomplish this and you'll look back on one your best hot summers yet.

What is 'Hot Sources of Heat'?

Heat has a couple of funny traits. First it is very much like age, you are comfortable where you are at, when you have been there a while. Much like being in your age bracket, being in a constant temperature becomes the norm, it is only when we move outside this that we experience distress. Heat is also like beauty; it can be 'in the eyes of the beholder'. What is hot for one is cool for another. I can attest for this, spending thirty years in the UK where the average summer high is 25c or 77f always felt reasonably hot. Then I moved to Sacramento in California and the temperature average that I had to deal with went to 32C+ or 90F+. Like all things training, I eventually adapted. Now UK highs feel cool and hot is 40C+ or 104F+.

We hear all the time "the heat doesn't bother me" which is a statement we certainly can't argue with. Your experience – perception is valid and real to you. But the fact that the heat doesn't bother you is a different statement than 'the heat doesn't affect you'.

Heat affects us all. It's really not something we can consciously control. That our body responds to heat is baked in the cake. It is somewhat analogous to saying "dehydration" or being "thirsty" doesn't' bother me. Again, maybe true but it does affect you.

Heat is the enemy of performance and endurance. During the summer months it surrounds you. As much as you try to avoid it and get used to it, the heat will catch up to you. Its effects can range from annoying and uncomfortable to fatal. Usually at a minimum it just takes away some of the inherit pleasure of riding your bike.

On a bright summer day your body is exposed to heat from three different sources and only one you can control.

- Confected heat from the road: Road surface temperatures can range from 46C/115F to 66C/150F+. Your body is only a few inches to a few feet away. You can bake on your bike.
- Radiant heat from the sun: Exposure to direct sunlight: Ultra-violate rays have an enormous effect on your perceived heat index. The same temp in the shade or in direct sunlight feels drastically different.
- Heat generated from your working muscles: Obviously, this is the one source of heat you control. And it's the first thing that drops when you're exercising in the heat.

Basics of physiology and thermoregulation
Consider your car. You drive around in the heat and you have no problems at all. Now consider turning your air conditioning off. Your car will still get you to your destination, but the experience will be completely different. This is the key focal point of this hot weather methodology. You are your car, if you make no adjustments to deal with the heat, then your body might still get you there, but you will certainly feel different.

"The harder your body works to cool itself, the faster you fatigue". David Carrozza.

Remember that the less your body has to do, the more it can focus on you cycling. Similar to riding on a full stomach or tensing your upper body too much, if your bodies thermoregulation is in overdrive, your cycling performance is being hindered.

The bodies way to deal with becoming too hot is sweating. Sweating is all about temperature control. When the body's temperature rises, the eccrine sweat glands kick into gear to keep our body temperature stable. Once the body passes 98.6 degrees, the brain's hypothalamus (the body's thermostat) goes off, and no, it can't just be turned down. This triggers the glands to release a salty mixture of water, sodium chloride, and other electrolytes. When sweat leaves the skin's pores, it evaporates into the air, taking some heat with it.

What is your sweat made of? 99% of it is simply water, with the remaining 1% a mixture of urea, uric acid, lactic acid, ammonia, vitamin C, electrolytes, and more about 760 different skin proteins.[lxvi]

So, it makes sense that a particularly long or hot ride increases the body's temperature and the need to start sweating. But, it's not just body temperature that causes sweating. During exercise, heart rate and blood pressure increase, which in turn cause the body to pump out more sweat. Plus, repeated exercises, like an interval session, can turn on sweat glands even without soaring body temps. Even when blood pressure falls after time on the bike is up, the body often keeps churning out sweat because the muscles stay stimulated.

Acclimation
The principle goal of any training programme is to prepare, or acclimate, your body to the conditions and demands of the event

you are partaking in. Of course, this has many features of components of fitness ranging from simply having the endurance to ride a bike for your target duration all the way to producing enough power on demand to win sprints, stage races, titles, medals, you name it.

What Spokes is aiming to do here is add the well-known, yet little discussed, element of heat into the equation. In the same way that you might travel to altitude for a few weeks prior to an event at altitude so your body can adapt to the thinner air, we want you to be capable of performing well at your event in the heat.

We also understand that you might not have the means or opportunity to spend around 14 days, prior to your event, on location and so have developed the methodology to reproduce said adaptation either indoors or out, the latter being weather permitting.

> *"Heat acclimatization (or acclimation) confers biological adaptations that reduce physiological strain (e.g., heart rate and body temperature), improve comfort, improve exercise capacity and reduce the risks of serious heat illness during exposure to heat stress.*
>
> *The biological adaptations include integrated thermoregulatory, cardiovascular, fluid-electrolyte, metabolic and molecular responses.*
>
> *Heat acclimatization occurs when repeated exercise-heat exposures are sufficiently stressful to invoke profuse sweating and elevate whole-body temperatures.*
>
> *Generally, about 1-2 weeks of ~90 min daily heat exposures are required; but highly aerobic fit athletes can heat acclimatize."* Key points from a Gatorade Sports Science Institute Study.

In practice this might look like utilizing indoor sessions to improve sweat rate (or more accurately, the timing of your body's sweating) and acclimating to heat, training to increase body temperature & then reducing heat during recovery periods.

Flatter rides outdoors; where power & speed can rise but the body might be capable of dispersing heat while there is sufficient wind. Interspersed with shorter hill reps; around half mile or 5% in gradient is ideal, where power can remain constant, or drop, but speed drops sufficiently for the wind to not produce the same cooling effect on our body temperature. Then, while in recovery interval, reducing temp as much as possible as well as heart rate to promote the body's ability to cool itself at high temperature, even when temperature isn't readily available.

Here's the best factor about forcing this type of adaptation, it will make you stronger in cooler temperatures too. A study by the human physiology department at the University of Oregon found that athletes who trained in hotter temperature, for a mere ten sessions, experienced up to 8% improvements over a controlled group training in normal temperature. The tests were conducted at the cooler temperature.

> *"The cyclists who were heat acclimated performed anywhere from 4 to 8 percent better than they had before they trained in the heat, while the control group did not improve at all."*

If forcing your body to acclimate to the heat sounds too much at any point and you feel you might be better off simply precooling (such as ice packs) you might consider that a study, on runners, by the Environmental Extremes Laboratory at the University of Brighton found that, while precooling got the athletes an additional 4% in performance against ignoring the heat entirely, adapting to the heat got them a 6.5% improvement. What would you do for an additional 2.5%?

"(1) The biggest benefit of heat acclimation may be plasma volume expansion. Just as altitude stimulates your body to produce more red blood cells, heat stress stimulates your body to produce more plasma. The result is a greater cardiac output, and higher VO2 at a given effort level. In the New Zealand study, resting plasma volume increased by 4.5%, even though the athletes had very high plasma volume to start; in the Oregon study, plasma volume increased by 6.5%.

(2) One of the key signals that tells your body to adapt may be dehydration. So, if you do the heat acclimation but are super-careful to stay hydrated, you miss out on the benefits. In the New Zealand study, the athletes were allowed 100 mL of water during the 90-minute bouts -- enough to stave off the feeling of being super-dehydrated, but not enough to stay hydrated. The benchmark some athletes are using: if you're not at least 2% dehydrated, you drank too much; 3% is good; 4% is too much. (Note: this is just for the heat acclimation sessions, not a universal rule for all training sessions!)

(3) This approach can be combined with altitude. Spend a couple of weeks up high to boost red blood cells, then a week in the heat to boost plasma volume, then maybe 7-10 days in normal conditions and you're ready to go." Alex Hutchinson, Runners World

Avoidance

We want to ask you a couple of questions here, should you avoid the heat and what happens if your event is hot?

One of the biggest coaching practices for dealing with training in heat has been avoidance of it. Perhaps that has been training at a certain time of day, finding shady rides, or just training indoors. While this might help produce a better response in the body for certain adaptations, it might not help you if your main event is in hotter temperatures.

This type of tactic dramatically limits training ability and the consequences of this might not support your overall objective. We would define this type of behaviour as a 'negative avoidance tactic'. Simply put, this is a damaging or limiting behaviour that helps you reach an immediate goal, in this case avoiding the heat, while damaging the chances of success at your overall goal, competing in the heat.

For those of us with busy lives, working, family and other commitments, planning to ride at a certain time of day might not be practical. We would argue that preparation for riding in the heat is better than avoidance, simple because you cannot always avoid the heat.

Aim to include more 'positive avoidance tactics'. These might look like finding loops close to a base so you can train in the heat but take regular 'cooling' breaks. Much like interval training at high intensity, where the recovery part is riding at low intensity, this broken-down approach to dealing with heat stresses the body less, allowing faster recovery and in longer term, better adaptation.

'Positive Tactics' will also look like adding devices such as Spruzza to your setup and helping your body lower its temperature using an external cooling system or source of water, much like dumping your bottle on your head, but in a more accurate and productive method.

Consequences

We are choosing to focus more on the consequences of heat rather than the extremities of being too hot, i.e. heat stroke and so on. Here we look at a combination of factors that overheating leads to and what we are aware is necessary in order to function at a certain level in the heat.

Firstly, is hydration or fluid intake. We would look to measure your fluid expenditure via testing, this might look like how much fluid is lost over a series of tests to determine and plot a graph of what intensity, related to time/power/temperature, you start sweating and then what quantity that is. Once we have that benchmark, we can look to utilize training to either adjust that sweat threshold through training or attempt to find those 'positive avoidance tactics' which you can use on the day of your event, see Spruzza. Spruzza equals lower dehydration; the same cooling effect of sweating, using an external source of water.

"Performance losses of dehydration might look like up to 30% reduced capability".

Secondly, is electrolyte replacement; which primarily comes from sodium. Again, measurable but only via a specific sweat test, Precision Hydration can provide this. Many people sweat different rates of sodium, failure to replace sodium might result in hyponatremia or in some cases this is similar to having too much water in your blood. This can have effects similar to dehydration. Knowing the density of sodium that you lose in your sweat arms you with the information to rectify it.

"The Central Nervous System and skeletal muscle systems provide important sensory input to the conscious brain, and there is evidence that each can play a role in impairing aerobic exercise performance during heat and/or dehydration stress. However, the demands and limitations on blood flow implicate a much larger performance contribution by the cardiovascular system." Journal of Applied Physiology, Vol. 109, No. 6, Mechanisms of aerobic performance impairment with heat stress and dehydration.

Preparation
While there might be ideal timing points for certain parts of this protocol the earlier you get started with this the better or more effective the results might be.

"Proper prior planning prevents piss poor performance"
The Seven P's, an old military adage.

Weather is not a requirement to utilize this protocol, indoor training can produce more accurate and specific results using a series of sessions to improve your body's sweat timing. Like mentioned at the beginning, the heat doesn't go away, but your body becomes better at dealing with it.

Remember we don't prepare for what is easy we prepare for what is hard and extreme.

"Expect nothing, prepare for everything."

The first steps to preparation start with self-assessment, a reflection on past experiences, challenges, successes and failures. How well have you performed in the heat before? Have you faced any specific challenges? What do you know about your training and racing that can be used to formulate a more effective programme for you?

Research & development
Insanity is described as "doing the same thing and expecting different results."

This phase is largely educational, and it involves explaining to the client the underlying science and principles behind the proposed changes in mind. Immediately following this comes a period of readiness to change and more self-assessment on the part of the client to change past behaviours, test new approaches and tools for improving.

Planning is a big part of preparation especially when change is involved. A coach here is invaluable. A coach will know what steps toward change will be necessary. But you should know what the benchmarks for assessing progress are, when you will reconnect to evaluate the effects, positive or negative, and how or when you will make corrections or decide to 'stay the course'.

Underlying preparation is the goal or goals for you and understanding the time and steps necessary for reaching them. It anticipates the time necessary for making midcourse correction accounting for adaptations along the way.

One of the strongest strategies you can add to your approach is to focus on eating healthily and treating your body well. An anti-inflammatory diet will help flush your body of free-radicals and increase the efficiency of all its systems including thermoregulation.

A diet, rich in fresh, locally sourced and organic produce will support this and start to reduce and repair the damage done to your body, on a microscopic level, by harmful free-radical cells. These cells are formed through normal day-to-day life and are increased when you add training into the mix.

Self-Assessment

Here we start with some information gathering. Among the necessary information you need to note down are key influencers such as history, current ability and goals. These will have a huge effect on just how you will personalise your plan.

In looking at your history, explore any recent riding achievements, milestones, knockbacks and experiences. Utilising tools such as TrainingPeaks, you can plot a graph of likely training growth from day one to the target goal or event. Where history indicates an experience which involves the heat, you will be able to pinpoint areas, specific to this package, which will need to be focused on.

In looking at your current ability, you are not necessarily looking at medical history, unless that is an issue, but an overview of both 'self-reported' training readiness and level of fitness. This may include where you live and ride, life circumstances and situations. A training diary, preferably hosted on TrainingPeaks, will provide enough background information on performance for you to make a start on tailoring your plan to your exact needs.

Some examples of health issues that predispose people to heat stress issues include MS, diabetics, women a few days ahead of their menstrual cycle, those suffering with low grade fevers and those taking certain medications.

> *"MS symptoms can become increasingly severe when there is an elevation in body temperature, with up to 80% of people with MS experiencing what is known as the Uhtoff's Phenomenon. This phenomenon is characterised by the temporary worsening of symptoms when the core body temperature increases by 0.5 degrees Celsius or more."* MS Research Australia.

Utilise a SMART approach to goal setting, go back over what you did in part one to see if you need to adapt anything. Are the targets being set Specific, Measurable, Attainable, Relevant and Time-Bound?

Armed with the information available you will be able to Truly Personalise your package to your exact needs.

Monitoring Effects
To ensure that you have progression throughout this methodology we have devised a number of ways in which you can both monitor growth and help improve your bodies thermoregulation.

Power Meters, HRM
Not only will you look to monitor your performance improvements to ensure your body continues to show positive adaptations, you might utilize methods in order to show that your body is coping better with the heat.

This might look like testing similar power outputs in extreme heat over a period of time to ensure that your heart rate doesn't spike, or that on longer rides you can push back or eliminate the point your heart rate spikes due to heat exhaustion and dehydration.

Each test should be individualised for you and your goals.

Sensors, Cameras
You might consider adding in infra-red sensors (IR) or core measuring devices to check that your body is becoming thermodynamically efficient.

Again, using similar testing protocol to that described above but this time focusing solely on whether parts of your body or core are remaining within the comfortable temperature boundaries for training and racing.

Pre & Post Weight Measurements
Simple yet effective. Pre and post weighing of your body to determine exactly how much fluid was lost within a certain timescale. This is an effective way of measuring how much you will need to hydrate in order to complete your event.

PH Sweat Testing
Precision Hydration have a couple of tests available to determine the amount of sweat lost in volume and then the quantity of sodium lost in that. The first is readily available online and although far less accurate will provide details about a recommended hydration and electrolyte supplement programme.

The second involves a non-invasive non-exercise test. Electrodes are placed onto the skin and a mild (so mild you can't feel it) electric pulse stimulates your glands into sweating. The resulting liquid is then analysed to give you an exact measurement of sweat volume and sodium quantity.

Lactate Tolerance Testing

Lactate threshold (LT) testing can be utilised to determine an appropriate training intensity and monitor progression in athletes of all levels. This test is similar to the VO2 max test, although consists of slightly longer periods of time between changes in workload. This test does involve several blood samples taken from the finger for the assessment of blood lactate. It is not considered a maximal test but does require a high-intensity effort.

Tied in with a similar additional protocol such as controlled heat we can see whether or not your lactate threshold is changing in response to an adaptation in your body's thermoregulation.

Self-Assessment Testing

A key part of this protocol will be your self-assessment using semi-quantitative self-reporting forms to record improvements and adaptations all specific to when completing training.

RPE – Borg Scale

This is a scale of 1-10 (some start is at a higher number and use 1-20, for this program we will use 1-10) where 1 is extremely easy and 10 is extremely hard.

PTI – Perceived Thirst Index

Again, we will use a scale of 1-10 where 1 is not thirsty at all and 10 is extremely thirsty.

PHI – Perceived Heat Index

1-10 where 1 is cool and 10 is extremely hot.

PFI – Perceived Fatigue Index
1-10 where 1 is no fatigue at all and 10 is extremely fatigued.

GIDI – Gastrointestinal Distress Index
1-10 where 1 is no distress at all and 10 is extreme distress.

HRV4Training Journal
Another key recording device for key performance indicators that will play a role in monitoring effects is Heart Rate Variability. This is very similar to the above but is conducted every morning upon waking rather than as a reflection of training. This is an app downloaded to your phone. First thing upon waking, you start by measuring your heart beat (pulse) for a minute then complete a list of questions to determine how ready you are to train again.

- HRV – pulse monitoring.
- Sleep quality (not necessarily quantity).
- Your thoughts on yesterday's training (easy, hard etc.).
- Motivational levels (in relation to your next training session).
- Your perception of your physical condition.
- Your perception of your mental energy.
- Your perception of your muscle's soreness.
- Your perception of your level of fatigue.
- Injury & sickness records.
- Your current lifestyle (unstable & busy or routine).
- Whether or not you did excessive traveling yesterday.
- Finally, anything else you feel relevant, notes on yesterday's diet and any supplements you have taken.

Pacing, Self-Assessments – Damage Control Reporting
Self-assessing is largely educational. What we intend to do is raise your awareness of what to assess. If you've ever heard anyone say "the heat doesn't bother me" they might be unaware of what is happening in their bodies during extreme heat. There will be no

dictating, just leading you to see and feel what is already there. We want you to feel that this works as a measure of its success.

To do this we will help you understand how intuitive reporting works. Simply put this is listening to your body and effectively reporting back what it is telling you. The previous chapter demonstrates the key performance indicators and their scales on which you will do this.

If you are unsure on how capable you are of self-assessing or you are somebody that routinely says "the heat doesn't bother me" I would strongly suggest looking into meditation or mindfulness training. A simple and effective way to do this is to download the Headspace app and complete 10 minutes per day. Once you complete the first three foundation packs move onto another, the 'Sport' packs are excellent and the 'Analysis' pack very relevant to this topic.

Once you are more aware of what your body is telling you, you might develop a greater understanding of what your body feels like when it is working and when to take a break. It is better to take a break than to quit entirely. The bigger the relationship you have with your body's own internal sensors the more accurate reflection your reporting will be. You will also find that pacing an effort becomes more reliable.

Not only will pacing be more effective but split testing will be too. A/B tests to validate your belief surrounding this HWP will help aspects to become more apparent. A simple example of this might be to follow what I did when first testing some of the features of the package out, including the Spruzza device. Head out on a ride, the first half hour using features of this package, then the second half hour without, ensure that the second half is equal to the first, power, HR, distance, speed and so on. After each section make a note of how you are feeling, what your perception is of the heat, the effort and your thirst.

Recovery

Here we talk more about the day-to-day recovery and general wellbeing of an athlete who trains significantly hard or in long durations.

Have you ever been out for a ride and been 'wiped-out' for the rest of the day feeling lethargic, extreme fatigue, irritable or anything else? What about waking up the next day with similar feelings? Did any of this affect your day-to-day life, work, family or anything else?

You'd be a severe minority if you told me no to every one of the above questions! What we want to demonstrate is that with proper focus on recovery you can have a significantly positive impact in your daily life too. This is why we refer to the HWP as an 'Ecosystem' integrated approach to training.

After testing Spruzza for a couple of weeks during the summer of 2015, Evan Huffman's first question was "You don't want this back, do you?" Evan went on to state, "Using Spruzza in the heat, I'm able to train harder and recover faster. I'm definitely feeling less fatigued after a hot ride.". Evan rides for Rally Cycling and has taken the KOM jersey at the Amgen Tour of California in 2016, two stages of the Amgen in 2017, plus overall wins in the Tours of Alberta and Gila.

You don't live in a vacuum with cycling being an independent, isolated activity. Training has to be integrated and coordinated with everything else in life. With correct usage of this methodology you can expect an increase in general wellbeing which might lead to you being a more productive person at work, more loving family member or a simply a healthier person to be around. With less feeling of fatigue, physically and mentally, you should see dramatic improvements in the work/family/training balance, or as I determine, the holy grail of amateur cycling.

Fatigue – Peripheral – Central Governor
When we talk about fatigue, we usually refer to simply our muscles getting tired, but there is another theory that might help us explain why we tire called the Central Governor.

> *"The central governor is a proposed process in the brain that regulates exercise in regard to a neurally calculated safe exertion by the body. In particular, physical activity is controlled so that its intensity cannot threaten the body's homeostasis by causing anoxic damage to the heart muscle. The central governor limits exercise by reducing the neural recruitment of muscle fibres. This reduced recruitment causes the sensation of fatigue. The existence of a central governor was suggested to explain fatigue after prolonged strenuous exercise in long-distance running and other endurance sports, but its ideas could also apply to other causes of exertion-induced fatigue.*
>
> *The existence of a central governor was proposed by Tim Noakes in 1997, but a similar idea was suggested in 1924 by Archibald Hill.*
>
> *In contrast to this idea is the one that fatigue is due to peripheral 'limitation' or 'catastrophe'. In this view, regulation by fatigue occurs as a consequence of a failure of homeostasis directly in muscles."* Wikipedia definition of Central Governor

Heat might also change the perception from central governor point-of-view. A study by the University of Canberra Research Institute for Sport and Exercise, Bruce, ACT, Australia, found that there were significant decreases in mean power output in the middle and end sections of paced efforts when under heat stress. The same study showed that with the use of pre-cooling methods there were no significant changes. The study goes on to suggest that *"negative feedback involving performance deception may*

215

afford an upward shift in MPO in the middle section of the trial improving overall performance. Finally, performance improvements can be retained when participants are informed of the deception."

The power of the mind.

Putting This Together
While this might initially seem quite daunting, you can simply start by some of the smaller parts. Maybe you're not likely to race in the heat but want to test out some heat adapted gains for riding in cooler weather. If you want to have a go, follow as many of the guidelines in the chapter as possible, then implement a training strategy. This might be something as simple as mid-intensity intervals (perhaps 80% FTP) indoors, without the fan being on. Start with short intervals and progress to longer. Depending on how hot your training environment gets, you might consider pre-heating the room too.

Part Four – Recap
If you have followed this part correctly, you will now have:
- Identified the need for any third-party help, such as coaches or bike fitters.
- Identified the need to upgrade or purchase any additional equipment.
- Created a tactical strategy for training, racing and competing.
- Identified if there is a need to and created your own 'Hot Weather' plan.

What next?

Congratulations! You've done it, all that is left to do is to go out there, implement your plan and be successful in achieving your goals. If you have been honest throughout this guide, made the right decisions suited to you (with no bias), and you have no outside influences effecting the event itself, such as injury or stronger competitors, you will achieve success.

If you have successfully completed what you set out to do, then again congratulations are in order! However, what do you do once you have reached your goals? You might react in one of two very different ways. On the one hand, you might feel an empty void that needs to be filled with another challenge, like a hunger to do even more and better yourself further. On the other hand, you might relax into everyday life, forgetting the awesome feat you have achieved and eventually detrain to the state you were in before you started your training. There is a middle ground, but in my experience, people tend to fall in to one group or the other. Among the athletes I coach, with those who race I'm already talking to them about their thoughts for next season part way through the current one. In fact, when I take someone on, I ask about their short, medium- and long-term goals (their goals one, two, four or even eight years ahead). Most people don't think as far ahead as eight years, but many do have some idea of what they want to achieve in a two- to four-year plan.

Go back and revisit the goal setting part of this guide, if you've achieved *everything* you set out to, then it is time to set some more! Unless you are thinking about retiring from cycling, resetting these goals is the best way to ensure you build on what you have already achieved.

But, what do you do if you have failed to reach your goals? First of all, you will need to consider why it was that you weren't successful. Did you over-reach? Was there some underlying problem that stopped you succeeding? Is it worth regrouping and having another attempt or do you need to be more realistic with your goals?

Maybe you got unlucky on the day, maybe you hit a problem in the journey. Maybe you are more motivated than ever to try again next year. But, be objective here, go through this guide again, specifically spending more time at the beginning, and see if you need to rethink your targets. But, identify your next goal as soon as possible.

Having that next step in mind is a huge motivator—if you hit a personal best in one season why not strive to beat it in your next? If you feel that you've hit the best you can achieve in one area, then you should travel farther afield. For example, why not do some international races? If you like to do Audax or Ultra-Distance, then you could think about aiming for a World Record attempt. Track riders could try the Hour Record for their age group. Sportive riders have the most fun as they can go anywhere in the world and enjoy different locations while succeeding in their discipline. The only limits you have are the ones you impose on yourself.

Read the next chapter for my personal experience on this subject...

Route 66

My Route 66 World Record attempt actually started in 2016. I was walking in Santa Monica, with one of my best friends, discussing my life transformation. When I was at my lowest, I was admitted to mental hospital, an alcoholic and an addict. I had gone from being told by doctors that I wouldn't be able to function as a member of society without mood stabilising medication, to owning a business operating in 20 countries around the world and winning multiple awards both on and off the bike. Damen, my friend, was adamant that this story would inspire others as much as it did him. After a while, I agreed and said that I would only share my story if I could tie it in with a way to raise money and awareness for mental health causes. At that moment we walked past the 'End of Route 66' sign on Santa Monica pier and the idea was born...

Fast forward almost two years and again I find myself stood by that sign. This time it was 4:45am and I was wearing my cycling gear. I had Thomas & Chris, my now good friends, there with me as I was about to embark on a 2500-mile journey across the United States. A terrible night sleep in a dodgy motel wasn't going to deter me, nor was the thought of battling out of Los Angeles traffic on Labor Day weekend. I was ready, excited and motivated.

Stage One
Stage One was the longest stage with some of the hardest riding you can do on a road bike. At over 240 miles, a mix between concrete jungle and desert, I knew it was going to be a long day. The LA traffic was actually non-existent, and we took scenic rides through Hollywood and Beverley Hills as we headed out of the greater Los Angeles area, which took us four hours, and into San Bernadino. As you can imagine, it was an interrupted ride. Stop signs, traffic lights and bike paths do not make for a fast ride. This left me already feeling disappointed that we would be behind my schedule. Each day I gave myself a two-hour cushion, which was to be used for stops, and in the event, I fell behind, the stops could

be shortened to bridge that gap. It meant the only way to keep on track was to be very efficient with time off the bike.

If you've followed my training journey, you'll know that I don't really like gravel. During the first stage of the Haute Route Rockies, I took a big fall on the first stretch of gravel. I needed stitches in my arm and many trips to the medical team to get my wounds cleaned. While I am open to conquering my off-road fear, I didn't expect there to be a half mile stretch of road work that left Thomas & I riding gravel (more like sand), with me skidding and swearing, and Thomas laughing. Thankfully, I made it across!

The pursuit of finding the most effective way to test my training led me to approach the Haute Route team. Initially I had hoped simply to ride their San Francisco event, it was geographically close, and the three-day structure presented a good test of the training I had been doing. I have ridden many events, from races to sportives to Gran Fondos, and nothing compares to the experience Haute Route provided. Police outriders, crossing Golden Gate Bridge and a time trial around Angel Island were just a few highlights of an event that had me craving more.

I was lucky enough to also participate in the three-day Asheville and seven-day Rockies events. The organisation of all these events is above anything I've ever experienced. I met people who are now my closest friends, visited some of the most beautiful places in the United States and tested my performance, giving me confidence that my body would sustain long, multiple days in the saddle. Haute Route truly is the pro experience for us mere mortals, the next best thing to riding a pro tour. If you get an opportunity to ride one, don't miss it.

Back on Route 66, and on the climb to Victorville, you have to leave the comfort of the frontage road and get on the interstate. If you've never ridden a road like this, imagine a five-lane highway with traffic moving at over 60 mph. The shoulder of I-15 was also a bombsite; you could probably build a replica vehicle with the debris left at the side of the road. Thankfully, I had Chris & Thomas in the car behind us with flashing lights and signage to warn other road users and we made the long trip up the mountain unscathed.

Once you finish the climb, you have, what you'd assume is, a pleasant downhill. Sadly, this is where the great state of California lets us down; the frontage roads are very worn with large gaps, rough road and a ride akin to the pave in Belgium. Many of the riders involved in my research, that had ridden Route 66, had commented that they thought about, or did, jump the fence and ride I-15 for the better surface. I didn't take this option; we have a route to follow and I had to follow that unless there was a significant reason to deviate from it.

Despite being provided with, arguably, the world's most comfortable bike, a Trek Domane, courtesy of William Sawyer Cars. I still took damage to all the points where my body made contact with the bike. For the remainder of the event I would be riding with both sore feet, hands and bum (well, that general region!), although my feet did make a recovery after a few days. There simply is no preparation you can do for this, not that will allow you to break the record. You couldn't ride a mountain bike or anything setup like that, you'd be too slow and there's no swapping of bikes unless there's a serious malfunction of the bike. I was already riding 32 wide tyres, it was brutal!

We had a solid finish to this ride as we made it into the desert, even with the heat making it harder in the afternoon. We were eventually joined by Luis & Alan, who were delayed, firstly by Luis' plane being cancelled and then by his bike going missing at the airport. They picked up 'The Meg', the RV loaned to us by Road Shark RV. 'The Meg' was fantastic. To have somewhere to rest each night and the sight of her each day at stops really motivated me, I can't thank Ed and Johnny enough. We all rode into Amboy, a ghost town in the desert together in the pitch black. Shake, shower, dinner, bed...

Stage Two
Up at 4:15am to be on the bike by 5am. I didn't feel too bad. Again, sleep wasn't the best, but from there on I'd sleep like a baby. The first obstacle of the day was the 10 or so bridges that were closed. We were faced with the choice of a long detour, and ride on the Interstate, or to try to force a way around them. I had no doubt that, given it was bone dry, I could walk around the bridges if I had to. We also knew that the car could double back and drive around if it came to that, so we pushed on.

The bridges were certainly closed to cars. But, after some manoeuvring and thought, we realised we could simply drive the car around too. Simple, so we thought, but, one of the final bridges wasn't even there, it had gone, with no way to ride it. So, like I had planned, I walked around. The loose, rocky surface was not easy to walk on and about half way around I twisted my ankle. I didn't feel any immediate pain, but I was quietly curious as to whether this would come back to haunt me.

After a stint back on the Interstate, now I-40 which we would follow in some form for most of the trip, we crossed the Colorado River. That was a sight to behold; amazing beauty in what had been such a barren landscape. We then headed deep into the Arizona desert where the temperature would be at its brutal highs in the 40's (with my Wahoo topping out at 50c). This day I was thankful for my Spruzza most, a small mister unit that sprays water into your face, this tool is a life saver! With barely any appetite, I was drinking nearly 1.5 litres of fluids every hour and still suffering. I wasn't able to enjoy the small town of Oatman as much as I'd have liked. This tourist trap with its stray donkeys might be the only place on Route 66 where tourism is affluent enough to keep businesses going.

Thankfully, as we headed back towards the Interstate, the heavens opened, and I got drenched. This was a welcome gift to cool me down, bringing me back to somewhat normality. We stopped in Kingman for some food, before Thomas & I headed back out to finish the last 75 miles. Almost another 240 miles in the bank today. Another late night, but still feeling very good!

Stage Three

We started and finished in Arizona today. After yesterday's predominantly desert day, it was nice to experience some of what the state has to offer at altitude. The first challenge today was major road work as we approached Flagstaff. Interstate 40 is not the busiest of roads, certainly nothing compared to Stage One's Interstate 15! It is mainly a route for long distance truckers, many of whom gave a supportive honk of their horns as they passed. We imagined that in the time we were following I-40, we probably saw the same trucker many times. Anyway, everyone seemed nice and content to give me as much room as they could.

However, and unfortunately, the road work reduced I-40's normal three lanes to one, meaning the truckers had no option but to pass by me close. Again, I have nothing but massive respect for the guys and girls who drive long distances. In the vast majority they all were courteous and moved lanes to give me room on the interstate shoulder. In this instance they couldn't do that. To make matters worse, for short periods, the wide shoulder was reduced to no more than a foot. Having semi-articulated trucks pass you, well within the three-feet law (no fault of the drivers'), was terrifying and I mentioned to Chris, who could no longer drive directly behind me to protect me, that if it got bad I'd bin the record attempt for my own safety.

Thankfully, it didn't last forever and, after Thomas joined me, we even managed to ride down to closed section, having the whole one side of the interstate to ourselves. With the wind with us, we were making good time and we even got to stop at an American

Diner, much to Thomas' delight! After that, and a quick mechanical stop to bleed my front brake, we left Flagstaff and headed towards the New Mexico border. With the wind with us we were flying, but, the shoulder of I-40 was another bombsite. Thomas had three punctures, which shortly followed by me blowing a tubeless tyre wide open too. I was riding a set of the ridiculously smooth Zed Bike Wheels; they glide well, and you can tell a lot of care goes into the hand building of each set.

After spending 160 miles on the interstate, I was glad when we turned off and headed towards Petrified National Forest Park. The area after leaving I-40 was what I was hoping to see, old single-track bridges and more remanence of what Route 66 was like before the interstate programme was brought in. You can really feel the soul of the road here. All the pictures I had seen while researching the trip, everything that filled me with joy and excitement was now right here in front of me. You really are able to retrace the steps of pioneers who made the journey between both coasts.

As darkness approached, we were heading into the National Park. Here we encountered one of the failings in my planning. I hadn't thought about park closure times and when we got to the gate it was shut. We could've jumped it and ridden on, but we would need to clear the park, nearly 30 miles, unsupported. This left us wondering if that was a risk too far. At worst, if we suffered a fatal mechanical, we would have to walk 15 miles in freezing conditions in the depths of the forest (it's worth a mention that it's no longer a forest and actually closer resemblance to the Grand Canyon).

With that in mind, we called it a night and parked up. It was during this stage my ankle had started to give me some issues, and when Thomas, our sports therapist, treated it I could tell he thought it was bad news. In the latter stages I asked him whether he thought I'd be able to continue on it, he said he was certain it was game over.

Stage Four

After losing over an hour the day before due to the park being closed, we lost a further hour to the park opening times at the start of Stage Four. Rather than our usual 5am start, we jumped the gate at 6am and headed off, knowing that the car would be able to come through with us at 7am. This already put us around 50 miles down on our target, something that was hard to comprehend given we had only really just started.

Petrified National Forest Park might be the most beautiful area I've ever cycled in, made more so by the sun coming up at dawn. I was lucky to share the ride with Alan, who I had met at Haute Route Asheville. Eventually we made it back to I-40, which we followed for around 70 miles, some on the shoulder and some on frontage roads. We even made a small navigational error upon approaching New Mexico and had to run across the interstate to get back on track. Like I said before, I'm just glad I-40 isn't the busiest of roads!

New Mexico was a place I was excited to see. I've never been to this state and the thought of seeing some of the extra-terrestrial heritage along the route was a nice reward! Gallup was our stop for lunch, a nice little city, where I was glad to see 'The Meg' for a brief break.

I prepared a lot of my food beforehand. I mass cooked my favourite bars; a mixture of oats, seeds, dried fruit & dark chocolate (100% dark), there is nothing but goodness in them. I then vacuum seal them for freshness and I ate about 5 squares a day. On top of that, we had bananas and other fruit, jerky, sweets, sandwiches and gluten/dairy free treats (I'm intolerant). I wanted to prove you could do a ride like this without 'sports food', it's not necessary at all. My hydration was provided by Precision Hydration, the only 'sports nutrition' product I would use. PH have tailored electrolyte strength for my level of sweating, that is volume of sodium lost. I used to suffer badly with cramp, I didn't get one episode during this trip.

After lunch I was delighted to be heading away from the interstate. But my delight was short lived when the heavens opened, and I got drenched. Now riding solo, I had no option but to push harder as, even wearing multiple layers, there was a real risk of hypothermia if I rode too slow. My power meter, a Stages model, had been intermittently working for a few days. The readings were well off and I think I set a new 60-minute power PB during Stage Three. I'm more than capable of riding to feel but having the meter to hold me back is beneficial, not that it was optional in this weather! After Route 66, Stages were very kind to replace my power meter, even though it was outside of warranty.

Thankfully, the thunderstorm didn't last forever and as soon as it dried up, I was joined by good friend, and client, Luis for a stunning ride through the El Malpais Wilderness Area. Our finish, in Grants, was again behind schedule and we were unable to make up the distance lost the day before due to the hour late start in the morning plus an hour lost to time zones. Arizona doesn't have daylight saving, so it meant we actually lost that time entering New Mexico. Being behind and having to get Chris to rebook RV parking was frustrating, given we were only on Stage Four. Not only that but this was a day where I rode slightly under a double century, two days in a row now and I hadn't planned for even one day less than 200. With us entering Texas tomorrow, we would lose yet another hour to time zone changes.

Stage Five
By this time, I had figured out that if I didn't flex my ankle, I was able to stop it hurting too much. With the help of some k-tape and pain killers I was able to keep pedalling, even if this might be somewhat reckless.

Today was an incredible stage, I look back at this as one of my favourites. Although Albuquerque, somewhere I really wanted to see due to my love of the television show 'Breaking Bad', was massively underwhelming. There was nothing bad about the city, it just seemed to lack character and anything of great interest. Thomas even asked me "when we would be heading through the downtown area", I replied "a few miles ago". It was an understandable question; I only knew because of the street signs.

The ride north to Santa Fe was incredible. Passing through the small town of Madrid, where the movie 'Wild Hogs' was filmed was amazing. You can almost feel the out-of-this-world energy. Probably in part down to the warning signs with little flying saucers above cows. Luis had joined Thomas and me. It was perfect weather, the climbing was stunning, and it was mixed with fun, fast descending.

Thomas and I found great amusement in appreciating the smaller things. Whether that is trying to get one of the many freight trains (many, many freight trains) to honk their horn, pretending to be motorbikes riding downhill or even the occasion where Thomas comes out of nowhere and scares the crap out of me on the interstate. All these factors added to the camaraderie the ride was creating between us all, I'm truly blessed to call the guys who made up the support team my friends.

The main issue with us following 'Bicycle Route 66', designed by Adventure Cycling Association, is that it does take you on all the tourist areas, even off the main route itself. I had opted to use this route for continuity, so the next person had a route that wasn't designed by me, something which could lead to bias. But it did mean taking odd trips to historic landmarks, just for the tourist value in it.

Catching up today was going to be hard. The planned stage was already nearly 230 miles, and we had now fallen around 50 down.

Finding new places to park the RV overnight was hard. Sure, we can dry camp at the side of the road or at a truck stop, but, then you have five people trying to use one bathroom. You also need to empty tanks and top up water/propane. You can get away with one night on the side of the road, but, too many and you need to stop the next day as well.

But it was a stunning ride to camp tonight, once you stray away from the busy roads there are so many smaller places full of character and history. Into Las Vegas, the New Mexico version, for the night. New Mexico didn't pull any punches in showing us how beautiful the scenery can be. Viva Las Vegas.

Stage Six
One of the least hiller days, this should've been where I started to catch up. After 45 miles of tailwind through the countryside we got back on the I-40, which we would follow for the rest of the day (almost 200 miles further).

If you want evidence of just how damaging to Route 66 the interstate programme was, visit some of the towns along this section. They are baron, almost wastelands. Every town is hopeful of one thing, tourists. But they all offer the same experience, so who is benefiting? In the years before I-40, these towns would have been prosperous places where weary travellers could rest their heads and find some food. Now they are desolate, devoid of any money and barely surviving.

Once you come down from the Rockies, you normally have a tail wind, of some form, from there all the way to Chicago. Named 'The Westerly's' it's only about one in every five years that it blows in the opposite direction. Thanks to the hurricanes about the make land on the east coast, this year would be one that bucked that trend and I was faced with 200 miles of headwind today with the prospect of over 1000 miles of headwind to come in the following stages.

That was sole destroying. I hate wind. But it was never going to be enough to make me quit. When we were on the frontage roads, the grippy surface and lack of vehicles made me wish I could get on the interstate, where there was an abundance of draft from passing vehicles. When I was on the interstate, I was unable to switch off for even a second, with the danger of hitting debris or the rumble strip meaning that I had to be mentally focused at all times. I wish I had the option of filtering between mental or physical exhaustion, but, following the ACA route, I was at their mercy.

The road surface was almost as bad today as it was on Stage One. Some of the roads during this trip went on as far as the eye could see. Sometimes this was ok, others like today, where you could simply see the hard-packed chip surface, were not. I was delighted to turn off one of these roads at one point, only to be thoroughly disappointed to find a gravel section lasting around five miles to follow. Again, Thomas behind in the car laughing, I crept my way to the frontage road by I-40.

New Mexico has a high clay content in its river beds, that turns a lot of its rivers red. While pretty and nice to look at, when faced with riding through it I had my concerns. One flooded section of the road, I sent the chase car ahead, to test the water and find a safe line. I could see by the movement of the car it was bad. I opted to run around the edge. While I didn't fall in, it did take a good five minutes to clear the clay from my cleats and that was the death of the Stages power meter.

It was during this stage that we had a call from Mathew, one of the support team we were due to meet in Oklahoma City. Mathew suffers with Sarcoidosis, an inflammatory disease and the reason I sometimes wear a purple version of my jersey. Mathew had been struck down with another episode and was hospital bound. He wouldn't be able to make it. I know he feels terrible about this, like he let me down, but all I wanted to know was that he was and would be ok.

I was very much looking forward to visiting Texas, another state I'd never been in. The border town of Glenrio would be a welcome stop for the afternoon. I enjoyed a late afternoon break before the final push. However, taken in by entering a new state, I missed the off ramp. No matter I thought, unlike the dual carriageways in the UK, where you can be on them for many miles before getting off, US roads typically have exits much more frequently. Ten miles later we pulled off at a rest stop...

We finished the day just outside Amarillo, one of the larger cities on the route, now 70 miles behind schedule, we were facing the prospect of needing to use an extra day to finish the attempt. That was ok, no one has ever followed Route 66 like I did on this ride. The closest before was a woman who did it in 23 days, but even then, I had a few people message me wishing me luck as this person had been falsely claiming the 'record' for many years. There was a Route 66 bike race one year, cancelled after multiple riders were hit by cars in Chicago. Many of the unaffected riders continued, but they were in groups. The only limit on our time was the support team needing to get back to their day jobs. It wasn't what I wanted but having to ride an extra day was looking more likely with every stage.

Stage Seven
This was the stage I was looking forward to most. The profile looks like someone literally drew a downward line from one side to the other. Around 230 miles of descending, granted there would be some lumps and the descent was actually only marginal, but it would be an easier day. It should've been an easier day. The wind put an end to that.

It was the right choice to not ride through Amarillo the previous night. At 5am the roads were quiet, but you could tell it would be slow when busy. We made it out of the city and off into the countryside, again, loosely following I-40 for the day. It was a gloomy day too, although I was sporting some extreme tan lines, mainly to the right side of my body (where the sun is most of the day), so I wasn't too worried about that.

I had developed a system to keep my mind focused each day. I tried to never think about how far in total I had to go. More how long until my next stop, how long until my next bar, how long until the next state, and so on. On top of this I had downloaded many audio books to listen to. Today I was listening to Bear Grylls' 'Mud, Sweat and Tears' a really motivating story about how he overcame adversity. Thanks for the encouragement, Bear.

Again, today there was very little to see here today other than towns struggling to survive. It was amusing to see the Tesla charge stations around here though. Given there was nowhere else to put them, they had to put them in a ghost town. If you've ever considered doing a road trip along Route 66 or wanted to ride certain segments, do it now, it's very hard to see how the businesses will survive. I presume they are run by diehards who want to preserve the heritage. Unfortunately, much like the towns they hope to preserve, they are all on a shelf life and I find it hard to believe there are too many people looking to spend their days running dead end businesses.

As we approached Oklahoma my spirits lifted. Every new state was one state closer to the finish. Again, with the headwind, we weren't going to make much distance up today, but, another solid day in the saddle with 225 miles covered. More importantly, mind and body were holding strong. Of course, it's a daily occurrence to have the "why am I doing this" thought. I usually deal with this by letting my ego take over, thinking about what people might say or think if I quit. Our egos can sometimes be incredibly damaging to our persona, but they can have their uses.

Stage Eight
Another stage I was really looking forward to. This marked the turn from travelling mainly east to travelling north-east. This was a

mental marker for me, almost like we were turning to head home, it was the last stretch.

Two big cities today, Oklahoma City and Tulsa, meant that in reality, we still might not bridge any of the distance we had lost, especially if those cities took time to get through. As we approached Oklahoma City my gear cable snapped. The bike had done well, but I was glad that both my mind and body had made it further than the bike. Forgetting the two slow flats and one blow out I had on the tubeless wheels, the bike had survived a lot! For a few days pervious I had noticed my shifting was sloppy. I simply put it down to it being dirty. Unfortunately, this wasn't the case my ride was halted.

Once I got on the spare bike, Oklahoma City was great, a real pleasure and the support we had from people was incredible. People asking questions at lights, honking their horns. My mood was at an all-time high today. Chris took the Domane to be fixed, big thank you to Al's Bikes for doing that so quickly and for the cost of the parts only. It was a revelation being back on my Madone though. I had ridden the Domane, setup mainly for comfort, for so long, that when I jumped on the other bike, in all its aerodynamic glory, it was a shock to be going so fast! I also had power back for the first time in a few stages and was pleased to see my effort was around my target power for each stage, 160 watts.

As we left the first major city of the day, we were riding busy back roads. This was a first for us, usually we were on quiet back roads, but now we were faced with having to manage traffic and not wanting to upset anyone. This was fine for a while, until the chase car got a flat. It's hardly surprising, you spend all day every day riding the gutter, or the dirty shoulder of the interstate, and you will inevitably get one. Somewhere we had gotten three nails in the tyre. I'm just glad it was this far in and wasn't repeated for the remainder of the event. This did mean that as soon as Chris brought my Domane back, he was off to fix the car. It also meant that I was now being chased by 'The Meg', the wide and long beast, which is less than suitable to chasing a slow bike rider on busy narrower roads.

As we approached the midway point in the day, I noticed a warm sensation in my right quad. Nothing like I had ever experienced before, I wasn't too worried at first and just kept on riding. I figured that I would have some issues along this event, that was a given, and as there was nothing I could do right then, I'd wait until my evening massage to address the situation.

As the light started to fade, we made it into Tulsa. Tulsa is an amazing city, very artsy and beautiful. I enjoyed none of it. My leg had gone from moderate burn to stabbing agony. I had no power through that side, not without more pain anyway, and now standing to relive pressure on my injured bum was also a problem.

Before I continue with Stage Eight, I wanted to mention the support crew, give thanks and explain how we came together as a group. For those who didn't follow my training journey, I had originally arranged for the support team to be made up of family and friends. The friends I had invited had, long before, told me that due to either finances or new businesses, they couldn't make it. While initially disappointed, I was respectful and understanding of their situation, at the end of the day it's not a paid job to support me and they have lives to return to after.

This presented an excellent opportunity to recruit some other people. Firstly, I had Chris approach me. Chris is an amazing human being, one of the most thoughtful and compassionate people I have ever met. We had only met the one time before Route 66, at Tour de Big Bear. We then had Thomas, from Altitude Training Cycling Camps. Thomas came on board as he would be in the US preparing for his gravel tours. He was more than happy to run my social media (a great job he did too) and offer support with massages in the evening. Mathew also offered to support the last four stages (Chris would take the first five). Mathew, a client like Chris, I met the day before I had my first date with Noelle, my wife. Mathew is another kind and generous person who I'm delighted to have in my life.

About two weeks before we were due to start Route 66, my father called me with some bad news. He had been diagnosed with cancer again and a more serious heart condition. He and my mother wouldn't be unable to travel to support. This was devastating for me. I now faced the fact that I would be supported by people I had met no more than once. While I am completely grateful and appreciate the efforts of the team, you can't replace people who have known you their whole lives. There is a bond that can only be built with time, something I look forward to building with the team, and that was a crucial part that was now missing.

This situation also left me with replacing two members of the team. First Chris stepped up and got unpaid time off work (thank you to Team Ford Lincoln). He would now be there from beginning to end. We then had Alan, who I mentioned I met at Haute Route Asheville, come into the fold. Luis, another client, also came forward. While no replacement for my parents, they provided me with amazing support throughout the trip. I've mentioned this many times before, but I wouldn't have gotten this far if it wasn't for their help. Thanks guys!

In the whole event I can only remember having two issues, the first was being fed gluten, something I'm intolerant too and leaves me with an upset stomach and skin complaints. The second was a misunderstanding on this stage. Around 150 miles in I was asked how far I wanted to ride today. I was feeling good, this was prior to the leg issue, and said I wanted to make some distance up today. A question was asked to me about how far I wanted to ride, I responded with an answer that would gain us maybe 10 miles on the deficit. Unfortunately, as we left Tulsa, it become apparent that rather than 10 miles to go, we had 30. This was a real low moment for me, I knew I was in trouble with my leg and having an extra 20 miles to do was not good news. But we pushed on.

Unfortunately, the situation didn't get better and in the small town of Claymore, we turned off the main road and headed towards our stop. I was again very frustrated (an understatement!) to find we would need to ride 4 miles off route to get to camp. 4 miles might not seem like a lot, but it really is a lot extra that you don't need to be doing. I opted not to get in the car. Getting in any vehicle is prohibited unless it is to move past an impassable object, this I didn't feel was characterised by that.

In my mind, when we finally rolled into camp and I could barely walk, this was the end.

Stage Nine
Thankfully, my leg felt better in the morning. I did, however, opt to get a ride to re-join Route 66, this would technically be an end to any official world record, although Guinness were denying our pleas to get the attempt recognised, saying it wasn't significant enough, anyway.

But, the thought of using the car, and the depression lingering from the night before, brought me to a standstill at a gas station around 20 miles into the day. I had given up. With Luis by my side, I sat down and drank a cup of gas station coffee. I text Chris and waited to be picked up.

It is at our lowest points where we are really tested. Do we sit and stare into the distance, never knowing what it would be like to try, or do we pick ourselves up and give it our best shot? After several minutes of meditation, thought and reflection, I got back up, jumped on the bike and headed off.

The wind had given me a break, the sun had come out and like a touch from the universe itself, I was revitalised. My energy and motivation returned, and I was flying with a smile on my face.

I got about 30 miles further into the ride before my leg started hurting again. It was manageable, but pain killers were no longer helping me. The thought of what the copious amounts of drugs were doing to my gut was frightening too. From that point, every 15 miles I'd need to stop and relax, but I pushed on to the century mark, where we met 'The Meg' just outside of Joplin and I sat to reflect.

Thomas and I went to work to see what we could find about the condition, whether it could be managed, and I spoke to a physio friend, it wasn't good news. What was almost certainly an elongated muscle wouldn't get better while riding and could lead to serious complications later on. The modified pedalling style, to protect my ankle, was coming back to bite me. Sure, I may have finished the stage in agony, but, three more stages would be out of the question. It's at times like these you need to be objective. One of the most powerful questions came from Luis, "what would I say if it was one of my clients?". My answer was fast and firm "I would tell them to stop". And that was it...

I wasn't as upset as I thought I'd be. I had given it my best shot. My body had lasted longer than the bike. My mind had lasted longer than my body. Of course, I had moments, even that morning, where my mind had thought about quitting, but I carried on.

This event was never about physical performance; it was about mental. The fact that I knew I could finish, if my body was well enough, was satisfying. It was a tearful live video I posted that afternoon to tell everyone the sorry news. But the support received was amazing. I know I couldn't do anymore, but I wasn't beaten.

The Aftermath

One of the strongest motivators for me was being able to ride with Chris in Illinois near his mother's grave. I was heartbroken that this wouldn't happen, it was his one wish and he sacrificed a lot to get it. I insisted that we still stop and pay our respects graveside. Then we went for an amazing dinner with his family. It was a warm and welcoming reception from them, something that characterises the American people.

There were two other items on the agenda; visit the Route 66 sign in Chicago and drop Luis off at the airport. After the first lay-in we had in over a week, we made this happen. I wasn't as tired as I thought I would be. My ankle was sore to walk on, but my leg was feeling ok. Mentally, it was hard to be at the Route 66 sign without being in my kit. Of course, I was disappointed, but I was motivated too. Even within an hour of quitting my event, Chris and I were planning the second attempt. That in itself tells you a lot.

One more night at a camp site near Chicago and we set off the following morning. A road trip that lasted about 30 hours to Las Vegas. 'The Meg' is a totally different beast when towing a car. To save two people driving, plus gas money, we rented a dolly and hitched up the car to the back.

I can remember being tossed around the bed in the back every turn Thomas made driving the RV up the Rockies in Colorado. We were all pretty disappointed that we made the Rockies at night, they are spectacular, and of course we missed it all.

We were all feeling pretty grim by the time we pulled in Las Vegas. A short turn around to get everything not needed off the RV and I drove the RV back home. If the theme of this trip was how big an influence the wind could be, it would be the same on the way back. Some of the wildest winds Nevada had experienced made driving the RV as difficult as it would be riding in it! I have even more respect for truck drivers who deal with that as part of their job.

Of course, it was great to be home. Home truly is where the heart is. For many nights, I would wake up and, dreaming, wonder where I am. I dreamt that I'd been riding all day and we were pulling into a new location for the night. It took me a while to recognise that I was in my home. I couldn't place why, I guess I have unfinished business...

Take Two
Yes, I'll be back. In terms of planning and execution, it went really well, and I have no doubt that, without the injury, I'd have succeeded. I would change somethings though.

Firstly, I do need one of any of the following people with me in support; my fiancé, mum, dad or best friends. It'll largely be the exact same team with the one addition. The extra one will double up as chef/nutritionist too. Something we definitely were lacking was a person who had nutrition, or at least my take on it, down. Having helped prep my food for years, either my fiancé or my dad would be perfect for that. Either of my best friends would be too, as they live my lifestyle and know exactly what I want and need. There is some truth to the myth that when you ride as much as I was you can eat anything. But I always ask my clients who ride a lot "do you want muscles made of cake or of something a little more substantial?".

We will also be more flexible with the route. The thought of facing as much headwind again is scary. If we could leave it until the last few days before the attempt and make a call based on current weather conditions, we could make the attempt far easier. It would mean the possibility of driving the RV all the way to Chicago to start, but we have to drive it both ways anyway. It could just be a rush to get started but I'd more than likely get a plane to ensure I wasn't already fatigued by the start.

We might throw the rule book out... If Guinness won't recognise it as an official record, then we could aim to just smash it! Allowing for change of bikes could mean that the faster interstate sections could be done on an aero or even time trial specific bike, we could use a lightweight bike for the hills and still have the comfortable bike for the harsh sections. We will see about this one, but it could be fun to see exactly how quick it can be done, and what a demonstration of what different types of bike can do.

I will also probably work out my own route. While the ACA Bicycle Route 66 is good and fun, there are significant gains to be had from not following it. We would need to see where this stood in terms of a record, but, cutting the tourist parts out and being more direct could shave a big portion. The detour for Route 66 takes you up to Santa Fe before returning back down, the original route followed this but was changed, taking this huge section out might shorten it by most of a day. I'll definitely plan the ride through Petrified National Forest Park a little better too!

One of the more disappointing elements for me was the amount I raised. Granted, I could not be more grateful for every penny or cent that people gave me. Every donation came from personal donations and I want to get more sponsorship from businesses. Given that the sponsors and partner companies got exposure of over 1,000,000 people, I think next year I should be able to get several large companies to put forth some serious cash to get their name next to mine.

The last thing would be testing some custom fitting clothing. I'll be looking into getting some clothing made specific to my size. I think there's definite comfort gains to be had from this. Nothing against what I have now, both the Direct Power Cycling Team and Assos shorts I use are great, but, after so many hours in the saddle it can still be uncomfortable. At least experimenting with this might add extra comfort.

For now, that's it! I'd like to thank everyone who has helped me get this far again. Feel free to reach out and get in contact, be you well-wisher, business or sponsor I'd love to hear from you.

Peace, out!

About the author

Pav Bryan is Co-Founder and Performance Director at Spokes (formerly Direct Power Coaching or DPC). Pav is also BikesEtc Magazines 'Cycling Guru', the resident coaching expert with his own back page feature. Pav is qualified to the highest national standard, a British Cycling level 3 coach, specialising in road and time trial. Pav is also a multi-time Kent Cycling Association Best All Rounder and 12 Hour Champion. He is a pioneer of client centric coaching, which promises the client a unique experience, one that they will be able to complete as well as enjoy.

Pav's love affair with cycling began at an early age, but as often happens, he lost touch with the sport in his teens and young adult life. Returning to cycle in his 20s, the sport became a tool in the quest to keep fit, active and healthy, and for enjoyment. When Pav joined his local club, Rye & District Wheelers, he was introduced to sportives and, ultimately, time trials.

In his first year of racing, Pav won the Kent Cycling Association (KCA) 12-hour time trial with a mileage of 269, not far off the course record. He also won his club's 10-mile and 12-hour championships.

In his second year of racing, Pav jointly won the KCA Best all Rounder, the combined average speed of best results from a number of events including 25, 50, 100 and 12-hour TTs. He was unfortunate not to retain his KCA 12-hour trophy due to a fall at hour six, but despite that, still finished second not far from his previous best.

In his third year of racing, Pav won the KCA Best all Rounder and the 12-hour trophies, having set a distance of just short of 280 miles. While Pav remains loyal to the Rye club, he will be riding for his own newly-formed club, Direct Power Cycling Team, for which he also holds the Team Manager position. A club that anyone can join for free, it is an online resource for anyone who wants to better their cycling. We have a paid version that comes with over 50 training plans, search 'DPCTeam' on Facebook for your free access.

Pav went to school at Robertsbridge Community College and left with 12 A-D grade GCSEs, before going to college at Bexhill to where he gained two A-levels; one in business and one in accounting. Instead of going to university, Pav chose to go straight into employment.

After almost a decade of working in various retail roles, Pav took a short period of time to pursue other interests before taking a part-time job as a Civil Servant to support the beginning of his own cycle coaching business. Cycle coaching was a natural choice for Pav, with his passion both for people management and the sport of cycling. He undertook the British Cycling Coaching qualifications and, in December 2015, completed the highest level attainable within road and time trial. He also gained certificates from Wattbike, TrainingPeaks, Fitness Genes and British Red Cross among others and is passionate about continuing to learn, with his sights set on gaining a degree at some point in the future.

Since starting his coaching business, Pav has been fortunate to work with many companies and he is currently an Ambassador for the Mind & NAMI charities. Pav enjoys working with clients of all abilities, squeezing every last percentage gain from high level athletes, alongside nurturing those new to cycling and helping them to improve from the moment they start working with him.

His love for nutrition has taken him to develop the Nutritionally Fit programme. Tailored for endurance athletes, the programme uses a combination of whole food nutrition, common-sense, easy-to-employ habits, incredible support and a wealth of resources to ensure that athletes recover quicker, have more endurance, and lose less time to sickness and injury. Thus, their performance gains become easier to attain. Nutritionally Fit is an open source anyone can access for free. It is funded by Pav and Spokes. Search 'SpokesNF' on Facebook for your free access.

Pav is also an advocate for changes in the way we treat and perceive those with mental health challenges. At a young age he experienced severe mood disorders, including anxiety, daily panic attacks, and was in his early twenties, diagnosed with Bipolar Affective Disorder. In August 2009, Pav was voluntarily admitted to mental health hospital where he was told he would never function as a contributing member of society without a concoction of prescription medication.

After spending several years working on his stability, Pav found the right combination of exercise, nutrition, relaxation and support he needed to come off of his medication. Today he manages a multi-national company with clients in over 20 countries. His journey with his mental health has inspired him to give back to others, yet to find their own stability.

In September 2018, Pav attempted to break the World Record for the fastest cycle ride of America's iconic Route 66, 2500 miles in under 11 days. Having ridden 1750 miles on a twisted ankle, his left quad succumbed to an elongated muscle a mere 500 miles from the finish and he pulled out. The ride was in aid of two charities, Mind (UK) and NAMI (US) – both do amazing work in their respective countries helping people through tough times towards mental stability. He raised over $7000.00 for both charities. In September 2020, Pav will do it all again.

It is this journey which has led him to think about each client as an individual and it was one winter evening in 2016 drinking coffee in Santa Barbara were the idea of Truly Personal Coaching was born.

Did you know?
It is not uncommon to double your power output when engaging a coach early on in your cycling life.

Why choose a Spokes coach?

Direct Power Coaching (DPC) had always been at the forefront of cycle coaching innovation and this has not been forgotten when DPC became Spokes. From the early days when Pav started the movement to making coaching more about the client. To integrating the latest technology, products or services within the coaching method. To a world first in incorporating a designer tool into his website so that athletes can build a training plan themselves. Spokes have always looked to be the leader in positive change within the cycle coaching community.

Spokes have always looked to be transparent and pay back to the cycling community through initiatives like Direct Power Cycling Team, the Nutritionally Fit programme or this self-coaching book. Since 2018, 10% of all client fees get donated to charity and Pav himself loves to donate his time to coach youngsters the art of riding for sport.

Pav has a network of coaches working with him covering all the main cycling disciplines and similar sports such as triathlon. All the coaches share and sign up to the Truly Personal Coaching ethos which ensures that every client that they coach gets a really unique experience. Every coach that works with him is fully qualified or is being supported towards that end. They will have extensive experience in the field of which they coach and proven results. Pav is proud to be mentoring an apprentice through the qualification process, and supporting the future coaches in the sport. Although taking the title Performance Director, Pav doesn't consider himself a boss, more of a leader and prides himself on heading a team and family alongside those he works with.

The coaches at Spokes really pioneer the Truly Personal Coaching method. They don't put the goals as the main influence of what your coaching looks like, they make it client-centric. Not only do they take into account your ability or capability, the time you have available, the demands of the targets, and any other influences, they also ask simple questions like how committed you are to reaching them. Unless you are a professional cyclist or are 100% dedicated to your goals, the coaches understand that, for most people, the journey is just as important as the end result.

You may have two or more important things in your life besides cycling, getting you to your goals is important but how much are you actually going to sacrifice to get there? What this book aims to do is to teach you how to look at yourself and truly tailor your own training to your needs and your commitment. We want you to enjoy your cycling as much as you do achieving your goals. This book will not replace the experience of a coach but will bridge the gap in your understanding of how to improve in cycling in a manner most fitting for you and the professional expertise of your chosen coach.

Acknowledgments

There are so many people in my life that I could thank, not just in the making of this book, but for making my journey possible. The support I have had over the years has been phenomenal. My family; both parents, brother and wife, have been instrumental in my success, both in writing this book and in life.

Without question, professionally, I'd like to thank everyone at British Cycling who coached and mentored me through their qualifications; Andy Kirkland in particular made me think more about my coaching style in a few months than I had in my life. You can't be a coach and not have been taught in some way by Joe Friel, Hunter Allen and Andy Coggan, I've not had the pleasure of meeting them yet, but have been fortunate to be interviewed by Cyclist magazine for a feature that included Hunter Allen, who has also been very complimentary about my coaching style and innovations. I'd like to thank them for shaping the way modern cycling training looks, is thought about, prescribed and monitored.

There are so many more people who have shaped my coaching style over the years, my parents who taught me how to communicate when I was a child, my teachers at school who furthered this and then the leaders who trained me in management and coaching as a young adult. I'd like to thank all my clients, past, present and future, for also determining my coaching philosophy.

I'd like to thank Nick Soldinger, Editor at BikesEtc Magazine, and everyone else at the mag, for giving me the opportunity to be part of the media industry.[lxvii] Thank you to everyone who has ever interviewed me, quoted me or helped me 'get heard'.

From a business point of view, I'd like to thank Andy Croft from Gilded Splinters, who for many years advised me on my marketing strategy and branding. My parents, in particular my father, have always been amazing business mentors, helping me setup and run my own DJ business as a young teen, to the advice still given to me as an adult. The coaches with whom I work and the others behind the scenes who help with my admin or have taken the time to help me when I've needed it. Paul Vines, my business partner at Spokes, who has helped me transform my business into something even bigger. I'm excited for the future of Spokes, changing the face of endurance sports coaching.

I'd like to thank each and every one of you for reading this book, I hope you have enjoyed it and will take away enough to transform your cycling. I'd love to hear what you thought.

To my step-daughter India, my little cookie, who is the drive and inspiration behind my need to better myself and help others. Finally, it is with lots of love that I give thanks to my wife and soul mate Noelle who I am truly grateful came into my life, a gift from the universe to keep me on the right path.

Bibliography

The information contained within this book has been built by my many years training to be a coach plus working and experimenting on my clients. Where applicable and available, references and further reading recommendations are made at the end of this guide.

Endnotes:

---

[i] For more information on creating a TrainingPeaks account please visit: https://www.trainingpeaks.com/athlete-features/

[ii] For more information on British Cycling, including help with terminology, please visit: https://www.britishcycling.org.uk/knowledge

[iii] Pav Bryan Blog: https://spokes.fit/blog/

[iv] Pav Bryan YouTube: https://www.youtube.com/pavbryan

[v] British Cycling Go-Ride club finder: https://www.britishcycling.org.uk/clubfinder

[vi] For more information on MyFitnessPal please visit: https://www.myfitnesspal.com

[vii] For more information on Strava please visit: https://www.strava.com

[viii] For more information on TrainingPeaks Annual Training Plan please visit: https://help.trainingpeaks.com/hc/en-us/articles/204073724-How-do-I-set-up-my-Annual-Training-Plan-ATP-

[ix] For more information on FTP please visit: https://www.physiology.org/doi/abs/10.1152/jappl.1988.64.6.2622. I also recommend reading the book: Training and Racing with a Power Meter by Hunter Allen and Andrew Coggan, PhD.

[x] For more information on the science behind cycling and triathlon training please visit http://www.jsc-journal.com/ojs/index.php?journal=JSC

xi For more information on muscle memory please visit: https://medium.com/oxford-university/the-amazing-phenomenon-of-muscle-memory-fb1cc4c4726

xii For more information on training at an 'older' age I recommend reading the book: Fast After 50, by Joe Friel.

xiii For a comprehensive look at power meters I recommend reading the book *Training & Racing with a Power Meter*, by Hunter Allen & Andrew Coggan.

xiv For more information on Training Stress Score (TSS) please visit: https://www.trainingpeaks.com/blog/what-is-tss/

xv For more information on the Borg scale please visit: https://www.hsph.harvard.edu/nutritionsource/borg-scale/

xvi For more information on Today's Plan please visit: https://www.todaysplan.com.au

xvii For more information on Golden Cheetah please visit: https://www.goldencheetah.org

xviii For more information on Facebook please visit https://www.facebook.com

xix For more information on Critical Power (CP) please visit: https://www.ncbi.nlm.nih.gov/pmc/articles/PMC5371646/

xx For more information in the TrainingPeaks workout builder please visit: https://help.trainingpeaks.com/hc/en-us/articles/235164967-Structured-Workout-Builder

xxi For more information on Zwift please visit https://zwift.com

xxii For more information on TrainerRoad please visit: https://www.trainerroad.com

xxiii For more information on Sufferfest please visit: https://thesufferfest.com

xxiv For a more detailed look at the importance of recovery in exercise I recommend reading the book Essentials of Exercise Physiology by William D. McArdle BS M.Ed. PhD (Author), Frank I. Katch (Author), Victor L. Katch (Author).

xxv Pav Bryan YouTube: https://www.youtube.com/pavbryan

xxvi For more information on RCUK please visit: https://roadcyclinguk.com

[xxvii] Reference the article by Ashley Quinlan in RCUK: https://roadcyclinguk.com/how-to/sleep-cycle-sleep-vital-recovery-performance.html#GPZ0kXm2y8z0x8Ul.97

[xxviii] For more information on HRV4Training please visit: https://www.hrv4training.com

[xxix] For more information on the British Cycling Coaching courses please visit: https://www.britishcycling.org.uk/coaching

[xxx] For more information on diabetes and cycling check out the work Team Novo Nordisk do: https://www.teamnovonordisk.com/manage-diabetes-exercise-part-1/

[xxxi] For more information on the role nutrition plays in exercise I recommend reading the book Sports and Exercise Nutrition by William D. McArdle BS M.Ed. PhD (Author), Frank I. Katch (Author), Victor L. Katch (Author).

[xxxii] For more information on the role genetics plays in nutritional needs please visit: https://www.fitnessgenes.com

[xxxiii] For more information on gluten problems in those without coeliac disease please see https://gut.bmj.com/content/65/12/1930

[xxxiv] Reference: https://www.ncbi.nlm.nih.gov/pubmed/26586275

[xxxv] For more information on fats please visit: https://www.health.harvard.edu/staying-healthy/the-truth-about-fats-bad-and-good

[xxxvi] For more information on micro-nutrients please visit: https://study.com/academy/lesson/what-are-micronutrients-definition-types-foods-importance.html

[xxxvii] For more information on the reduction in nutrient density among produce I recommend reading the Journal of the American College of Nutrition, www.jacn.org;

[xxxviii] For more information on the Atkins diet please visit: https://www.atkins.com/how-it-works

[xxxix] For more information on gluten problems in those without coeliac disease please see https://gut.bmj.com/content/65/12/1930

[xl] Reference: https://ghr.nlm.nih.gov/condition/lactose-intolerance

[xli]Reference: https://www.ncbi.nlm.nih.gov/pmc/articles/PMC2714380/

[xlii] For more information on cramping please visit: https://www.scientificamerican.com/article/what-causes-leg-cramps/

[xliii] For more information on the Precision Hydration Sweat Tests please visit: https://www.precisionhydration.com/pages/sweat-testing

[xliv] For more information on Hyponatremia please visit: https://www.ncbi.nlm.nih.gov/pmc/articles/PMC4470176/

[xlv] Reference: https://www.ncbi.nlm.nih.gov/pubmed/10198142

[xlvi] For more information on Aeroponics please visit Tower Garden

[xlvii] For more information on the role of sleep in athletic performance visit: https://www.sleepfoundation.org/sleep-news/sleep-athletic-performance-and-recovery

[xlviii] For more information on Feng Shui visit: https://en.wikipedia.org/wiki/Feng_shui

[xlix] For more information, please visit https://www.headspace.com

[l] For more information on the chemicals in your water supply please visit: http://freshlysqueezedwater.org.uk/waterarticle_watercontent.php

[li] For more information, please visit: https://thinkup.me

[lii] Reference: Self-affirmation activates brain systems associated with self-related processing and reward and is reinforced by future orientation. Christopher N. Cascio, Matthew Brook O'Donnell, Francis J. Tinney, Matthew D. Lieberman, Shelley E. Taylor, Victor J. Strecher, and Emily B. Falk.

[liii] Reference: https://www.ncbi.nlm.nih.gov/pmc/articles/PMC419707/

[liv] For more information on why you should hire a coach, visit here: https://www.cyclingweekly.com/fitness/why-everyone-needs-a-coach-23201

[lv] For more info on my Training Plans, visit here: https://www.trainingpeaks.com/coach/pavbryan#trainingplans

[lvi] For more information on Dartfish please visit: https://www.dartfish.com/sports

[lvii] For more information on Coach's Eye please visit: https://www.coachseye.com

[lviii] For more information on sports psychology, I recommend reading the book The Chimp Paradox by Dr Steve Peters.

[lix] Check out https://spokes.fit/product/mental-fitness-coaching-programme/

[lx] Although it might not shed much light on your own performance, I really loved reading Sean Yates' book 'It's All About the Bike'.

[lxi] For more information on Infinity Bike Seat please visit: https://infinitybikeseat.com

[lxii] For more information on Brooks saddles please visit: https://www.brooksengland.com/en_us

[lxiii] Reference: https://www.ncbi.nlm.nih.gov/pubmed/12840640

[lxiv] Reference: https://www.ncbi.nlm.nih.gov/pubmed/17218899

[lxv] For more information on Spruzza, please visit: http://www.spruzzamist.com

[lxvi] For more information on perspiration please visit: https://en.wikipedia.org/wiki/Perspiration

[lxvii] For more information on BikesEtc Magazine please visit: https://bikesetc.co.uk

If you've enjoyed reading this book and would like to further your knowledge, then I would recommend the following titles.

Training Bible by Joe Friel (Velopress, ISBN 9781937715823) *The Cyclist's Training Bible is the bestselling and most comprehensive guide for aspiring and experienced cyclists. Joe Friel is the most trusted coach in the world and his proven cycling training program has helped hundreds of thousands find success in the sport. Joe has completely rewritten this new 5th Edition of The Cyclist's Training Bible to incorporate new training principles and help athletes train smarter than ever. The Cyclist's Training Bible equips cyclists of all abilities with every detail they must consider* *when planning a season, lining up a week of workouts, or preparing for race day.*

Training and Racing with a Power Meter by Hunter Allen and Andy Coggan (Velopress, ISBN 9781934030554) *Power meters have become essential tools for competitive cyclists and triathletes. No training tool can unlock as much speed and endurance as a power meter--for those who understand how to interpret their data. A power meter displays and records exactly how much energy a cyclist expends, which lends unprecedented insight into that rider's abilities and fitness. With the proper baseline data, a cyclist can use a power meter to determine race strategy, pacing, and tactics. Training and Racing with a Power Meter makes it possible to exploit the incredible usefulness of the power meter by explaining how to profile strengths and weaknesses, measure fitness and fatigue, optimize workouts, time race readiness, and race using power.*

The Chimp Paradox by Dr Steve Peters (ISBN-10: 039916359X/ISBN-13: 978-0399163593, May 30, 2013) *Do you sabotage your own happiness and success? Are you struggling to make sense of yourself? Do your emotions sometimes dictate your life? Dr. Steve Peters explains that we all have a being within our minds that can wreak havoc on every aspect of our lives—be it business or personal. He calls this being 'the chimp', and it can work either for you or against you. The challenge comes when we try to tame the chimp, and persuade it to do our bidding.*

Essentials of Exercise Physiology by William D. McArdle BS M.Ed. PhD (ISBN-10: 1608312674/ISBN-13: 978-1608312672) Essentials of Exercise Physiology *offers a compact version of the* Seventh Edition *of the bestselling* Exercise Physiology: Nutrition, Energy, and Human Performance, *making it ideal for introductory undergraduate courses. As students' progress through the text, they will develop a deep understanding of the interrelationships* among energy intake, energy transfer during exercise, and the physiologic systems that support energy transfer. Moreover, they will discover how to apply what they have learned to enhance exercise training, athletic performance, and health.

The Hour by Michael Hutchinson (Yellow Jersey Press, <u>ISBN 0-224-07519-5</u>) *Full of fascinating tales, The Hour is the story of one man and his bike against the clock in the quest for pure speed and an attempt to add his name to the list of record holders in the only cycling contest that matters.*

Faster - The Obsession, Science and Luck Behind the World's Fastest Cyclists, (Bloomsbury, <u>ISBN 9781408843758</u>) *For professional cyclists, going faster and winning are, of course, closely related. Yet surprisingly, for many, a desire to go faster is much more important than a desire to win. Someone who wants to go faster will work at the details and take small steps rather than focusing on winning. Winning just happens when you do everything right—it's the doing everything right that's hard. And that's what fascinates and obsesses Michael Hutchinson. With his usual deadpan delivery and an awareness that it's all mildly preposterous, Hutchinson looks at the things that make you faster—training, nutrition, the right psychology—and explains how they work, and how what we know about them changes all the time. He looks at the things that make you slower, and why, and how attempts to avoid them can result in serious athletes gradually painting themselves into the most peculiar life-style corners. Faster is a book about why cyclists do what they do, about what the riders, their coaches and the boffins get up to behind the scenes, and about why the whole idea of going faster is such an appealing, universal instinct for all of us.*

Time-Trialling. Fly Through the Pain Barrier: Achieve Your True Potential in the Race of Truth! By Adam Topham *The four fundamentals of flying are lift, drag, thrust and weight. Take* *away lift and you almost have* Time-Trialling. *Reduce drag, increase thrust or power, reduce weight and you are on your way to learning how to fly on your bike! The fourth fundamental is pain! Just as insufficient lift will keep a plane from taking off, insufficient pain will keep a time triallist from truly flying. Here is your fast track to all those little and not so little secrets your rivals don't want you to know about. Avoid the common mistakes and misconceptions that disrupt or limit the development of many riders. Avoid the expense and frustration of trial and ERROR! Read about how to get the most out of yourself and your equipment. Achieve your true potential. Fly through the pain barrier!*

If you want to learn more about coaching, contact British Cycling and take some of their qualifications. TrainingPeaks and Wattbike also have some excellent ones that will help you understand what your data means.

Made in the USA
Middletown, DE
13 October 2020